John Laffin is widely regarded as one of the world's leading authorities on contemporary Islam. He has travelled widely in most of the 44 Islamic countries and knows those of the Middle East particularly well. Dr Laffin is the author of more than 100 books, 15 of which in one way or another concern Islam. Another 50 are about military history and war. A broadcaster, lecturer and novelist, Dr Laffin is based in Britain.

By the same author

Middle East Journey
Return to Glory
One Man's War
The Walking Wounded
Digger (The Story of the Australian Soldier)
Scotland the Brave (The Story of the Scottish Soldier)
Jackboot (The Story of the German Soldier)
Tommy Atkins (The Story of the English Soldier)
Jack Tar (The Story of the English Seaman)
Swifter Than Eagles
The Face of War
British Campaign Medals
Codes and Ciphers
Boys in Battle
Women in Battle
Anzacs at War
Links of Leadership (Thirty Centuries of Command)
Surgeons in the Field
Americans in Battle
Letters From the Front 1914–18
The French Foreign Legion
Damn the Dardanelles! (The Story of Gallipoli)
The Australian Army at War 1899–1975
The Arab Armies of the Middle East Wars 1948–1973
The Israeli Army in the Middle East Wars 1948–1973
Fight for the Falklands
The Man the Nazis Couldn't Catch
The War of Desperation: Lebanon 1982–1985
Brassey's Battles: 3,500 Years of Battles, Campaigns and Wars
On the Western Front (Soldiers' Stories From France and Flanders)
Western Front 1916–1917: The Price of Honour
Western Front 1917–1918: The Cost of Victory
War Annual 1 1985–86
War Annual 2 1986–87
Battlefield Archaeology
The Hunger to Come (Food and Population Crises)
New Geography 1966–67
New Geography 1968–69
New Geography 1970–71
Anatomy of Captivity (Political Prisoners)
Devil's Goad
Fedayeen (The Arab-Israeli Dilemma)
The Arab Mind
The Israeli Mind
The Dagger of Islam
The Arabs as Master Slavers
The P.L.O. Connections
Know the Middle East (An A–Z Reference Book)

JOHN LAFFIN

Holy War
Islam Fights

GRAFTON BOOKS

A Division of the Collins Publishing Group

LONDON GLASGOW
TORONTO SYDNEY AUCKLAND

Grafton Books
A Division of the Collins Publishing Group
8 Grafton Street, London W1X 3LA

A Grafton Paperback Original 1988

Copyright © John Laffin 1988

ISBN 0-586-06868-6

Printed and bound in Great Britain by
Collins, Glasgow

Set in Caledonia

Contents

CHAPTER ONE

Face to face with Holy War

American marine sentries on duty outside their Beirut base early on the warm morning of 23 October 1983 noticed a typically battered Lebanese truck approaching the gate. They were not alarmed; the truck had only one occupant, the driver, and he was smiling.

As he neared the gate the driver picked up speed, jinked his truck around a few barrels set as a barrier, and with his foot hard down on the accelerator rammed the vehicle into the Marines' five-storey building.

In a shattering roar 2,000 lb of explosives blew up, the building collapsed into rubble and 241 Marines – most of whom had been asleep – died in the wreckage. Minutes later a second suicide truck-bomb rammed into the French paratroops' base close by and 58 paras died. Both suicide drivers were blown to pieces.

The attacks shocked a world already horrified by years of atrocities in Lebanon. The sentries on duty at the gate were more appalled than anybody else – they were the only ones who had seen the driver. 'But the guy was smiling,' they said in a tone of bewilderment to every journalist who came to the scene. The point was written into the Marine official report of the event – 'The guards stated that the driver was smiling.'

'Jeez, a guy doesn't smile when he knows he's going to die . . . does he?' one Marine said. He felt sick and guilty about allowing the truck to enter the base, though as his automatic rifle was unloaded – the officers didn't want 'accidents' – he could not have stopped it.

A week later I was in the ancient town of Baalbek, Lebanbon, to interview a man who had largely helped to organize the attacks on the Americans and French, Hussein Mussawi, leader of a group of Shi'a Islamic fundamentalists. In his early forties, Mussawi (or Moussavi) is an intense, intel-ligent-looking man with a thick, short-cropped black beard and drawn-in cheeks. We sat in the sun outside a stone building in which he had an office, and a half-circle of similarly bearded and intense men, all younger than Mussawi, gathered close by. Fixing me with his staring dark eyes, he calmly explained why the Beirut attacks had been made. 'It is really very simple,' he said. 'We are at war with the Americans, who are enemies of Allah.'

I asked what made them enemies of Allah? That too was simple; Ayatollah Khomeini had declared them to be so. Mussawi said that he had nothing on his conscience and commented, 'Many more Americans, French and others will die.' He was proud of the events in Beirut.

I passed on the question from the Marine in Beirut – Why was the suicide attacker smiling as he went to certain death?

'Because he was also going to equally certain Paradise,' Mussawi explained. 'Having killed enemies of Allah he became a martyr beloved by Allah. *Of course* he was smiling.'

'Would *you* drive a truck-bomb and blow yourself up with it?'

'Of course,' Mussawi said again, and he obviously meant it. 'Death in the name of Islamic holy war is the purest form of sacrifice.'

'How long is this holy war likely to last?'

'Until all the enemies of Islam are overcome, one way or another,' he said. 'The Holy *Koran* promises that this will happen but it may take years.'

In 1982 Mussawi had broken away from Nabih Berri's Amal (Arabic for hope) organization to found Islamic Amal. He made it clear to me that his own group and others are at holy war with certain Muslims, as well as Christians and Jews. 'Many Islamic states have failed to live up to the ideals of their religion,' he said. 'In particular Saudi Arabia and the rotten Gulf sheikhdoms. Even Sudan and Pakistan have made serious criminal compromises in their eagerness to accommodate Western interests. They will recognize the error of their ways – and sooner rather than later.'

Mussawi kept returning to the theme of the spiritual force that guides Islam, speaking with strong feeling but without raising his voice or lapsing into vehement rhetoric, as Arabs tend to do. He was all the more impressive – and all the more frightening – for his calculated answers to my questions.

He spoke about Ayatollah Khomeini with great affection and respect. 'The great Ayatollah,' he said, 'has shown the world what the masses can accomplish when they are strongly motivated by a spiritual force. I personally am always regenerated by his inspirational presence.'

Eleven days after the Beirut bombings, on 4 November 1983, with the help of other Islamic groups, he sent another suicide truck bomber to attack the Israel Border Police HQ in Tyre; 60 people, the majority of them Muslim, were crushed to death in the explosion. On that occasion the driver was shot dead but his bomb-on-wheels still hit the building. This reminded me of something else that Mussawi had said, 'Now that jihad is in motion nothing can stop it. Nothing.'

Its surviving victims are aware of its implacable violence – those maimed in explosions, held hostage during hijacks, tortured as enemies of Allah. Many of its victims have died, some with agonizing slowness.

In May 1985 I came face to face with the horror of holy war in the Shouf Mountains, east of Beirut. These are beautiful but dangerous hills, divided on tribal and religious lines between Lebanon's Maronite Christians and Druse. In times of conflict it is difficult to know which faction controls any given area; even those who live there move cautiously and usually in strength in certain places. An error of judgement can be fatal. It *was* fatal for the man whom I saw suspended on the wall of a ruined building, which had probably been wrecked by a Syrian shell.

Crucified on the wall, in the traditional 'Jesus' fashion, he was desiccated, his corpse held together by his clothing. Pinned to his chest was a notice, scrawled in Arabic, French and English so that the message would be clear to all. It read: *This will remind him of Jesus Christ*.

That he was Christian was evident – a crucifix dangled from his neck, outside his shirt. His murderers could have been Druse, Iranians or Shi'a Muslims. I had come across a victim of Islamic holy war and an eye all too experienced in the ways in which men die violently told me that this one had died slowly and painfully.

His limbs had gone rigid in the middle of a contortion of pain, so that his fingers were clenched and his body was bent sideways at the waist. He was obviously in Muslim territory – had he died on his own ground his friends would have removed him. He was just one of something like 100,000 Lebanese – from all the country's religions – who have been killed since 1975.

The purpose of this book is to explain what jihad or holy war is, where it came from, how it wages its campaigns, the inducements it offers its warriors, why its planners consider themselves at war, how it chooses its enemies and where it is going.

Failure to understand holy war makes all of us – the Communist-atheist East as much as the Democratic-Christian West, and all the political systems

and religions in between these two great hemi-
spheres-of-influence – all the more vulnerable.

The high degree of vulnerability became apparent at Vienna and Rome airports on 27 December
1985 when Palestinian terrorists attacked with
grenades and rifles the queues of people waiting at
the airports' El Al check-in desks. They killed 18
and wounded 118. The massacres were carried out
by the 'Martyrs of Palestine,' yet another holy war
group, one led by the arch terrorist Abu Nidal.

Jihad – the holy war of Islam – is the greatest
political-religious force of the late 20th century and
its commanders-in-chief are determined that by
the year 2000 of the Christian era Islam will have
regained its 'rightful place' as the dominant world
system.

CHAPTER TWO
Declaration of War

Jihad is not a *secret* war. Those who wage it might keep their tactical objectives and their operational plans hidden but they announce both the onset of the war and its strategic objective. If their enemies have not heard it then they have not been listening or they have discounted it as rhetoric. Rhetoric comes naturally to Islamic leaders but they are deadly serious in the basic message they present.

Ayatollah Khomeini first declared his holy war while plotting the Iranian revolution to overthrow the Shah during the 1970s. Even during his years of exile from Iran his declaration was disseminated by cassettes sent from Paris and broadcast in the mosques. With the Shah deposed and anarchy prevailing, Khomeini further stressed the state of war when his *Pasdaran* or Revolutionary Guards seized the American Embassy in Teheran on 4 November 1979. To show the seriousness of his purpose he held the diplomats hostage for 444 days.

In the history of jihad, 14 January 1980 was a significant day. A party of 120 Pakistani army officers visited the holy city of Qum, in Iran, and were presented to the Ayatollah. In stern tones the never-smiling dictator lectured them for three

hours about their duties as Muslims in 'an unholy
world.'

Finally, he said: 'We are at war against infidels.
Take this message with you – I ask all Islamic
nations, all Muslims, all Islamic armies and all
heads of Islamic states to join the holy war. There
are many enemies to be killed or destroyed. Jihad
must triumph.'

Jihad is not, as popularly imagined, merely
Islam's war against the Christian West and against
the Jews. It is also aimed at all Muslim monarchs,
as monarchies are anathema to strict Shi'a Muslims.
Other enemies are 'reactionary' Islamic regimes,
such as that of Egypt, and those Muslims declared
to have betrayed Islam. This category includes the
majority of Sunni Muslims, who are considered to
be heretics by Shi'a Muslims. Other major enemies
to be fought in modern holy war include the United
States – described as 'the Great Satan' – Israel, and
all non-Muslim states which offend 'God's messenger'. In modern times the Messenger – in effect
the successor to the Prophet Muhammad – is
Ayatollah Khomeini or his heir. President Gaddafi
of Libya, who has declared himself to be the Mahdi
or 'Expected One' to lead Islam, regards his opponents as enemies to be destroyed in holy war.
President Zia of Pakistan, a major Islamic country
in size and influence, is just as insistent on the
eventual triumph of Islam but for him the principal
'infidels' are the Hindus of neighbouring India. As
the builder and custodian of the 'Islamic bomb'
Pakistan is accorded particular respect by the Arab-

Islamic nations. A Pakistani general is the author of the standard Islamic textbook on holy war – *The Koranic Concept of War*.

Khomeini's imperious call to holy war rang throughout the 44 nations of the Muslim world and many Sunnis as well as all Shi'as were stirred by it.

Jihad is a multi-faceted form of warfare, more genuinely a 'total war' than that conceived by the Fascist and Communist leaders of the mid-20th century. It means armed struggle and battle; it also means war through economic and political pressures, through subversion and propaganda, through conversion of non-Muslims to Islam and through penetration of non-Muslim societies. Translated, jihad means 'a great striving' and it calls for relentless and remorseless action worldwide.

All Muslim scholars and commentators strongly make the point that *qital* (fighting and waging war) – the word is often used in the *Koran* – is the highest form of jihad.

In December 1979, the month after the seizure of the American Embassy, the Great Mosque at Mecca was the scene of a dawn ceremony to mark the beginning of a Muslim new century, 1400. It was well attended and among the crowd were 500 holy war warriors with weapons hidden among their robes. Heavily armed, well trained by Yemeni instructors and backed by Iranian ayatollahs the insurgents took up key positions with the objective of capturing the mosque. This was as great an act of sacrilege to devout Muslims as an

attack on Jerusalem's Church of the Holy
Sepulchre would be to Christians or an assault
against the Western Wall to Jews.

In violent fighting throughout the vast building,
Saudi Mosque Guards killed more than 300 insurgents, including their 'spirit' Muhammad al-
Quraishi, who called himself the Mahdi – the
'expected one' of Islam. A theology student, al-
Quraishi was a Khomeini follower. All those attackers taken prisoner were beheaded.

The mosque attack was another manifestation of
holy war. It was 'holy' in the eyes of the conspirators because the Saudi royal family, the guardians
of the greatest of Muslim mosques, is 'corrupt' and
must be deposed. By staging their coup in Mecca,
the holiest of all Islam's holy places, they hoped to
spread holy war faster.

While the conspiracy against the Saudi royal
family was being hatched the Saudis themselves
had been proclaiming holy war. In November 1979
the Saudi Minister of Wakfa (religious trusteeships)
demanded a holy war against Israel. His call, while
speaking to a world conference of Muslim theologians, was reported only in the Arab press, including Arab-language papers in Israel.

In August 1980 the publicity given to jihad was
world-wide because this time the call for a 'long,
relentless, pan-Islamic holy war' against Israel
came from Crown Prince Fahd of Saudi Arabia. In
Mecca, the birthplace of Islam, Fahd solemnly
faced the Kaba – the small temple within the
grounds of the great mosque – and sent his dra-

matic call throughout the Muslim world and beyond.

Prince Fahd's statement looked like an effort to keep the royal family in position to resist militant religious and political elements within Saudi Arabia and placate Saudi's large Palestinian bureaucracy concerned about fellow Palestinians in the occupied territories and in Lebanon. Fahd seemed to be speaking to the larger Gulf region, fully conscious of the rise of Iraq after the fall of the Shah in Iran. It was significant that earlier that month President Saddam Hussein had paid an official visit to Saudi Arabia, the first by an Iraqi head of state since the fall of the monarchy in Iraq nearly 20 years before. The Saudis needed to keep up their credentials with the hard-line states, not only because of shared Arab goals but in order to influence the others.

Saudi Arabia took its call for holy war to the world Islamic conference in Fez, Morocco, in September 1980. The Islamic foreign ministers agreed to plan jihad against Israel for its formal annexation of East Jerusalem. Their 24-point 'final declaration' declared: 'Islamic countries have an obligation to proceed with a full jihad, regarding it as resistance in every political, economic and cultural field, together with its military aspects.' At the same conference Syria and the Palestine Liberation Organization demanded a 'general mobilization for jihad' in all Islamic countries but the conference stopped just short of this step.

The Saudis pressed their jihadic call. In the first

few days of October 1980 their foreign minister,
Prince Saud al-Faisal, said, 'The kingdom of Saudi
Arabia has no other recourse but to call for jihad
for the sake of establishing the supremacy of righteousness and justice and eliminating falsehoods
and injustice.'

By now the Saudi jihad was aimed not only at
Israel but at Egypt as well, for having made peace
with Israel in what history now knows as the Camp
David Accords; against Libya, because it con-
demned the Saudi royal family as reactionary;
against Iran, because its leaders were working for
the downfall of Saudi Arabia; and against Afghanistan, whose leaders were in league with the athe-
istic Soviet communists.

While the Saudis had been pressing for jihad so
too had Gaddafi – but *his* holy war was against
Saudi Arabia. In the same formal way as Prince
Faud, though from a greater distance, Gaddafi
faced towards Mecca and the Kaba and proclaimed
jihad. 'This country will be liberated from the evil
rule of the royal family of Saud,' he said in September 1980.

On 6 October 1980 President Anwar Sadat of
Egypt sat among Egyptian dignitaries, foreign
ambassadors and special guests in Cairo stadium to
watch his army pass in review before him. He was
proud of that army because it had fought well in
the 'Great Crossing' – the war against Israel in
1973. On that bright day he was, in effect, saluting
his fighting men for having given him his greatest
military triumph.

While Mirage jets on aerial display screamed over the parade ground and wove coloured vapour trails, six blue-bereted soldiers led by an officer leapt from an artillery vehicle lumbering past the saluting base. First they lobbed grenades and then they opened fire with their Kalashnikov rifles. One dashed across 30 metres of open space until almost within point-blank range of President Sadat. Before the president's guard could react, Sadat had been hit by five bullets and 30 other people had been killed or wounded.

Sadat, one of the most courageous statesmen of history, was a victim of holy war. He had been sentenced to death by Khomeini, Gaddafi and the leading ayatollahs and imams, including many in Egypt. They had the tacit approval of the Saudi régime, despite the enmity between the Saudis and the extremist Khomeini and Gaddafi.

The execution was planned by a major of Egyptian army intelligence, Abud El-Zomor, who recruited the killers. In their eyes Sadat was guilty of two offences. The first was that he had become 'an enemy of God by making peace with Israel, a nation of infidels.' In Islamic jihadic terms the attackers were not murderers but soldiers of Allah, willing to become martyrs for the passionately held belief that they must kill his enemies. Sadat's other offence was that he had liberalized Egyptian society by freeing it, to some extent, from the grasp of the Islamic fundamentalists who wanted a return to the strict precepts of Islam.

The third Islamic Summit Conference on

Palestine and Jerusalem, held at Taif in Saudi
Arabia 25–28 January 1981, seemed to endorse the
need for Sadat's murder. Without directly referring
to Sadat and Egypt, 38 Muslim heads of state and
Yasser Arafat representing the Palestine Liberation
Organization proclaimed jihad against Israel. Iran
and Libya, although absent, had already made their
support clear.

Only four months later, in May 1981, the
attempt on the life of the Pope – the symbol of
Christianity to the vast majority of Christians – may
indirectly have been one of the consequences of
the call to holy war. The would-be assassin was a
Turkish Muslim.

In March 1982 the Islamic holy war against the
non-Muslim world was more definitely formalized
at a conference held in the Independence Hotel
(formerly the Hilton) in Teheran. Nearly 400 men
with credentials as revolutionary ideologists, as
practical revolutionaries and as religious leaders,
met to give Khomeini's holy war in particular and
Islamic jihad in general public approval. This was
felt necessary to show that it was not just Khomeini
alone who was calling for jihad but Islam as a
whole. The conference ended with a declaration
that, under the guidance of those present, 'Islam
will launch a large-scale offensive to cleanse the
Islamic world of Satanic Western and Eastern
influences that are hindering its progress. Simultaneously, Islam will cleanse itself of undesirable
and unholy elements.'

Events in the holy war continued in December

1983 when a truck-bomb badly damaged the United States Embassy in Kuwait and five remote-controlled bombs blew up Kuwaiti installations. The explosions gave clear warning that the oil emirates of the Gulf were in danger of being crushed between two holy wars – that directed against the United States and its Western allies and that taking place between Iran and Iraq. The 'Gulf War' was begun by Iraq in the hope of a quick victory and capture of disputed territory. For Iran it rapidly became a jihad and hundreds of thousands of Iraqis and Iranians have perished in the conflict. The Iranian casualties included tens of thousands of children who had been so profoundly indoctrinated that they willingly rushed into enemy minefields to explode the mines with their bodies to clear paths for their army's tanks.

Because of the intensity of religious feeling it generates, Islamic holy war has a momentum of vengeance which makes the world its battleground. The French learned this on New Year's Eve 1983 when an express train travelling from Marseilles to Paris had a carriage torn apart by a bomb. Another bomb damaged Marseilles railway station. The two bombs killed five people and wounded 30. Warriors for jihad had struck again. The French Press explained that the Islamic Jihad Organization 'admitted responsibility'. In Iranian newspapers the wording was quite different; here the Islamic Jihad Organization 'claimed the victory.'

The attacks on the American Embassy in Kuwait and on the express train were minor incidents compared with the events in Beirut on 23 October 1983, which I have already described. It was no coincidence that these attacks were made during the period of Muharram, the holiest time of the year for Shi'a Muslims.

Despite the violence in France and other places, in the Western world holy war is generally waged with less open violence but books about Islam frankly reveal the will for conquest. One of the most significant publications is *Jihad – a Ground Plan*, written by Abd al-Qadir as-Sufi ad-Darqawi and published, in English, in Britain.[1] Abd al-Qadir is direct: 'We are at war. And our battle has only just begun. Our first victory will be one tract of land somewhere in the world that is under the complete rule of Islam . . . Islam is moving across the earth . . . Nothing can stop it spreading in Europe and America.'

Sheikh Zahra, a leading Muslim theologian in Cairo has proclaimed: 'Jihad is not confined to the summoning of troops and the establishment of huge forces. It takes various forms. From all the territories of Islam there should arise a group of people reinforced with faith, well equipped with means and methods; and let them set out to attack the usurpers, harassing them incessantly until their abode is one of everlasting torment . . . Jihad will never end . . . it will last to the Day of Judgement. But war comes to a close as far as a particular group of people is concerned. It is terminated when the

[1] By Diwan Press, 1978.

war aims are realized, either by the repulse of aggression and the enemy's surrender by the signing of a covenant or by permanent peace treaty or truce in favour of Islam . . .'

Abd al-Qadir and Zahra both echo Khomeini, who wrote while in exile in Paris: 'Holy war means the conquest of all non-Muslim territories. Such a war may well be declared after the formation of an Islamic government . . . It will then be the duty of every able-bodied adult male to volunteer for this war of conquest, the final aim of which is to put Koranic law in power from one end of the earth to the other.'

Khomeini has also said, 'The person who governs the Muslim community must always have its interests at heart and not his own. *This is why Islam has put so many people to death: To safeguard the interests of the Islamic community. Islam has obliterated many tribes because they were sources of corruption and harmful to the welfare of Muslims.*'[2]

By prescription and tradition, holy war is war without scruple and it is fought until victory is achieved. Truces may be arranged but their purpose is to gain some advantage, such as time; a treaty arranged with an infidel may be legitimately broken.

Violent events of the type I have described are carried out as a form of theatre so as to gain publicity but not all holy war campaigns or actions are fought so overtly. The missionary mullah who

---

[2] Author's italics.

converts pagan black Africans to Islam is as worthy a warrior as the soldier or the Kalashnikov-carrying priest. Islam's more academic theologians, such as those at Al-Azhar University in Cairo, claim that ten million Africans embrace Islam each year. They are the fruits of the 'great striving'.

Wherever the strict rules of Islamic law are imposed – as they were in Sudan in 1983 – the leaders of fundamentalist Islam applaud and reward the ruler responsible, even when they oppose him on other grounds. His actions, when in conformity with Islamic law, are proof of the great striving for Islam. So too are coups brought about by economic pressure. For many years an embargo on oil supplies from Islamic countries was a weapon of holy war. In 1985 a complete reversal took place – certain Islamic states threatened to glut the market with oil, thus bringing down the world price and causing panic among oil producers and dealers. The mere threat to cut oil supply lines is a jihadic weapon. During 1985 Iraq strove to reduce the flow of oil from its enemy Iran, in the hope that the US and Western Europe and Japan – who buy Iranian oil – would feel compelled to intervene in the war and force a peace.

The great striving of the late 20th century did not spring from one Iranian ayatollah's fanatical anger and his zeal for 'reform'. Nor from one Libyan colonel-president's ambition to lead the Islamic world against the West. It is the product of more than 13 centuries of Muslim history.

Jihad will not simply wear itself out and it is not

'going through a phase,' as some Western people hopefully believe. It is steadily building towards a plateau of climax and it demands to be understood.

At the same time the Islamic concept of revolution must be understood. Because Western people do not understand it they have a built-in handicap when trying to analyse the great new force of the 'Islamic Revolution,' which has inspired holy war.

In Western thinking revolution is connected with development and progress; the French Revolution and the English Industrial Revolution are only two of the more famous examples. We speak of 'computers causing a revolution in industrial science' and of 'satellites producing a revolution in communications.' Always we mean that progress has occurred.

An Islamic revolution is necessarily retrogressive because its aim is to get back to the values and attitudes of the time of the Prophet Muhammad, and to return to his example. In Islamic thinking, the Islamic revolution comes round every one hundred years. It was for this reason that Ayatollah Khomeini declared his revolution precisely at the turn of the 15th Islamic century. In doing so he not only threw out the Shah's 'ungodly' régime but demanded a return to the Islam of Muhammad.

The Western mind conceives revolution as producing something fresh and new – even if it is not always admirable or comfortable. For Muslim revolutionaries the new and the novel are abhorrent and diametrically opposed to holy teaching, which stresses the importance of the traditional.

For Islamic teachers, academics and fundamentalists revolution is not accidental. For them human history is cyclic, thus revolution is part of the divine order and everything in the world is governed by an inexorably moving wheel of fortune. The ideal is to keep this wheel moving so that one fixed point on it will return to the perfection of Muhammad's time. It is certain to come, despite opposition to it.

This is precisely why that very opposition must be fought and defeated. It is the force which will not permit the wheel of fortune to complete its revolution. Those who comprise this enemy are Great Satans, imperialists, colonialists, missionaries, Zionists, Christian infidels, Baha'i infidels, Muslim apostates and enemies of Allah. The irony of this is that very few of them realize why they should be considered enemies.

It is really very simple. In one way or another they have created 'change.' And in Islam revolution means reversing any change that may have taken place. Holy war is rather more complex. To understand jihad it is necessary to go back to its roots in the Arabian desert in the 7th century.

CHAPTER THREE

A *hot breath from the desert wastes*

In the year 563, seven years before the traditional year of birth of the Prophet Muhammad, a famous Arab chief, Harith, travelled to Byzantium to see the famed and feared Emperor Justinian of the Greek Christian empire. He carried with him a written declaration of his own faith, which was sharply opposed to the orthodox belief. He wanted Justinian to listen to it.

The mass of Arabs were pagan or polytheists. However, Harith believed in one god and with some Arabs rejected the Christian concept of 'God the father, God the Son, God the Holy Spirit.' One sentence in his letter is characteristic of Arab defiance of Christianity. 'The so-called Trinity is false; there is only one Divinity, one Essence, one Nature. Those who will not accept this doctrine must be despised and hated.'

Justinian was more amused than angry by Harith's temerity in challenging Christian authority but the bishops of Byzantium were furious and refused to endorse Harith's declaration. He said ominously, 'Now I know that you are heretics. We and our armies accept this doctrine, as do the orientals. In time, so will you.'

Harith was making a claim and a threat. The claim was to the possession of a native Arab religious

belief, the threat was to defend it and spread it with
the sword. It was the initial hint of Islam, the first
hot breath of jihad from out of the Arabian desert
wastes.

From the very year of his birth Muhammad's name
was associated, in Islamic teaching, with military
conflict. Mecca, his birthplace, was a pagan centre
whose religious life was based on a small temple
called the Kaba, the Arabic word for cube. Set in
the corner of the Kaba was a black stone, said to
have fallen from heaven and therefore sacred. For
long years before Muhammad the Kaba had been a
shrine to the many gods and idols of wood and
stone worshipped by the Arabs. Once a year the
Bedouin tribes made a pilgrimage to Mecca, where
they walked around the Kaba, worshipped the idols
and bought supplies in the market place of the
thriving trading town.

About 550 miles south of Mecca lay the city of
Sana, in Yemen, governed by the Christian,
Abraha, for the Christian ruler of Abyssinia. Abraha
had two reasons for wanting to humble the Meccans: To defeat them as trade rivals and to make
his own Christian city of Sana, with its fine cathedral, more illustrious than the pagan Mecca. He
found a pretext for war when two Meccan Arabs of
the Fuqaym tribe committed an act of sacrilege in
Sana cathedral. He led an expedition north along
the Red Sea coast to punish the whole of Mecca
and took with him an African war elephant, a beast
never before used in warfare in Arabia.

No fighting occurred because Abraha's army was afflicted with smallpox and had to retreat. Later the *Koran* would say of this episode: 'Have you not considered how Allah dealt with the Army of the Elephant? Did he not foil their stratagem and send against them flocks of birds which pelted them with stones . . . ?' This was an allusion to the pockmarks on Abraha's soldiers.

Thus, to Islam the failure of Abraha's campaign was willed by Allah, who protected his house, the Kaba. The time became known to the Meccans as Am al-Feel, the Year of the Elephant. After the birth of Islam and the rise of Muhammad the fact that he was born in that particular year was accorded great significance. So too was the nature of the invading enemy – a Christian army. But even in 570 Christianity was discredited by Abraha's 'defeat' and Christian hopes of converting all Arabia abruptly ended.

Muhammad – the name means 'worthy of praise' – was born into the Beni Hashim, an inferior clan of the Kuraish tribe, a few months after the death of his father. Kuraish mothers usually sent their babies out to women of a Bedouin tribe to be nursed; Muhammad's mother, Amina, sent him to the Beni Saad, where he stayed for six years. His mother died less than a year after his return home and the orphan Muhammad was cared for by his grandfather for the next two years until he too died. Muhammad was then taken into the family of his uncle, Abu Talib, and went with him at the age of 12 in one of the great trading caravans to Damascus.

At Bosra, then a major city, south of Damascus, Abu Talib presented Muhammad to a famous Christian monk, Bahira, who is said to have foretold that the boy would have a great future. During the years to come Muhammad was to meet other men, who, like Bahira, worshipped one god.

He was also deeply influenced by a particular oath-taking in his youth. Muhammad attended a meeting called by the eldest uncle and head of the family to found an order of chivalry, the Hilf al-Fudal, whose members swore to aid any other member oppressed in Mecca. Muhammad eagerly took the oath and later, after his recognition as the Messenger of God, he would say, 'I am not prepared to surrender this honour . . . and even today if anybody calls me for help in the name of this order I will run to his aid.'

Muhammad grew up as a trader, illiterate but able and apparently respected. At the age of 25 he became an overseer for Khadija, the widow of a rich Meccan merchant, and led her caravans on trading missions to Syria. In 595 Muhammad and Khadija were married and Muhammad became an important man in Mecca. It was one of Arabia's major urban centres, a base for complex commercial business and international trade, a hub of routes leading to the Mediterranean. An enemy who wished to control the city had only to block the Meccan caravans.

By the age of 40 Muhammad was spending a

period each year in a lonely cave on Mount Hira,
near Mecca. It was here, in religious contemplation, that he experienced a vision of the Angel
Gabriel, who addressed him as 'the Messenger of
Allah – or God.'[1] All that he heard in this and later
revelations Muhammad learned by heart and in
time the material was written down and became
the *Koran*.

His first followers in submission to the will of
Allah – that is, Islam – were Khadija, Ali his cousin,
and Zaid a slave boy, soon to be joined by a trader
friend Abu Bakr and some young people of Mecca.
Khadija died in 619 and by then Muhammad had
about 200 followers, all of them in danger from the
aroused and hostile Meccans. In March 620, under
conditions of great secrecy, Muhammad met 12
men from Yathrib, another pagan town, about 200
miles north of Mecca. At this meeting, known as
'first Aqaba' because it took place in a little dry
wadi of that name, the Yathrib men promised to
worship only one god and to obey Muhammad as
his messenger.

The martial *nature* of Islam – as distinct from its
later actual belligerency – may be said to date from
March 622 when Muhammad met in rendezvous
73 men from Yathrib. These men had decided to
join Muhammad's religion. This was a dangerous
decision and they came through the night along
different trails and in twos and threes to avoid
being seen. In the cold air at midnight they sat

[1] He was not known as the Prophet until after his death.

before Muhammad who after an address asked them to swear allegiance to him; in effect this meant an undertaking to protect him when he visited Yathrib. The 73 men filed past Muhammad in the gloom, each one striking his hand against that of Muhammad in the Arab token of loyalty. Then Muhammad cried out, 'I am of you and you are of me! I will war against those that war against you and I will be at peace with those who are at peace with you!' After choosing 12 leaders the Muslims dispersed. The pledge they had made, known as 'the second Aqaba', not only established Islam but one of its main principles – jihad.

The situation in Mecca had become critical for Muhammad. In the year 622 the Angel Gabriel warned him that his life was in danger and that it was time for him to leave. This flight on 16 July 622, the Hegira, begins the time-scale of Islam – Anno Hegira (A.H.) 1. Yathrib became Medina-al-nabi, city of the prophet.

Soon after his arrival in Medina Muhammad drew up a form of constitution. Its most important provision was that, for the first time, loyalty to the tribe or political confederacy was replaced by loyalty to a community of religious believers. It was a momentous concept since it drew a line between Dar al-Islam, the land of Islam, and Dar al-Harb, the land of war. In Dar al-Harb were all those who rejected Allah and his Prophet; they were therefore considered to be in a state of enmity with those of the true faith, Islam. This distinction was never

amended or suspended and is as strong thirteen
centuries later as it was in Muhammad's lifetime.

In making a pact with the people of Medina,
Muhammad's principal aim was to unite the Jews,
Muslims and atheists of Medina against the idol-
worshippers of Mecca. The Angel Gabriel brought
an order: 'Fight the idol-worshippers.'

This was a declaration of war. Arab Muslims say
that Muhammad had no zest for war and Islam
universally believes that Muhammad never killed
a man with his own hands, though the Muslim
guides at the Topkapi Palace in Istanbul, where his
bow is preserved, talk of Muhammad's arrows
having struck the enemy at the battle of Badr in
624.

To Muhammad the Meccans were idolaters and
they had cast out Allah's invocation to war.
Muhammad raided their trade caravans, not
merely to capture much needed booty but as part
of a strategic policy to consolidate his position in
Medinese society.

A *Koranic* revelation further urged the Muslims
to 'contend' with their pagan enemies – the very
first incitement to holy war. The prelude to 'con-
tention' was reconnaissance – probing missions
designed to intimidate the Meccan caravans and to
find out their strength. Then in January 624
Muhammad sent Abd Allah Hajash with 12 men on
a mission so secret that he carried a sealed letter to
be opened after two days' march. In it Hajash
found orders to proceed to Nakhla, between Mecca
and Taif, and there to attack a Meccan caravan.

One man in the caravan was killed and the Muslims returned to Medina with rich booty and two captives. The affair was nothing more than a skirmish but it had taken place during a sacred month when Arabs did not fight. This caused an outcry and the breach of ethics worried the conscience of even Muhammad's most devoted followers.

At first Muhammad denied responsibility for the deed, saying that his orders had been misinterpreted. It was only in a later revelation, when he had been aroused by the sight of the rich loot, that he declared war against 'unbelievers' and justified division of the spoils – even in the holy month. The relevant *Koranic* reference is 2.214: 'They will question you (O Muhammad) with regard to warfare in the sacred month. Say: "Warfare therein is a serious matter but to turn men from the way of God and to disbelieve in Him and in the holy mosque and to keep his people from it is more serious with God, and infidelity towards him is more serious than killing."'

Muhammad's decision to wage war in the holy month is still being justified. In his book, *The Origin and Development of Islam*, 1980, the Pakistani author Asghar Ali Engineer, says: 'The verdict was very clear. If the people of Mecca obstructed the new faith and movement, retribution would be exacted and traditions would not be allowed to stand in the way. No movement which aspires to establish itself as a power can succeed without breaking old traditions and adopting strategies designed to suit the exigencies of the situation.'

The Meccans, alarmed by Muhammad's belligerence and his attack at Nakhla, mustered a thousand men to convoy their next caravan, in the summer of 624. Muhammad, with only 300 men, forced them into battle on ground of his own choosing, south-west of Badr. Before the battle he prayed in a small tent and emerged reciting a *Koranic* revelation: 'Soon shall the hosts be routed, and they shall turn their backs.' The importance of this utterance during the centuries which followed cannot be over-estimated.

The Muslims were already disciplined and determined and Muhammad made them more so in a fighting battle speech. 'The victory depends neither on pomp and pageantry nor in abundance of weapons. What is needed most for victory is patience and steadfastness.' Full of enthusiasm for their new faith, the Muslims were convinced of the justice of their cause. Unlike the Meccans they now had a unified command. Even more important, they had no compunction about whom they might kill.

One of Muhammad's most impressive achievements was in convincing Arabs that jihad as a sacred duty was more important than the loyalties of blood relationship. His first practical step was to persuade the Medinese to attack their old friends of Mecca with whom they were linked by marriage – as well as commerce and the ancient pilgrim rites. Also he had to induce the Meccan emigrants to take up arms against their heathen kinsmen and, if necessary, kill them. To overcome the age-old tradition of never spilling common blood was a considerable psychological victory. The new religion had no tribal boundaries and it was permissible for a man to kill even his own father on the other side. The son of Abd Allah Ubayy asked Muhammad's permission to kill his father for his 'treachery' towards Muhammad. It was necessary for him to be his father's executioner; had anybody else killed him the son would have had to seek blood vengeance.

At Badr the Meccans advanced behind their three banners and Muhammad, seeing them appear over the sand dunes, shouted, 'O Allah, here are the Kuraish in their vanity and pride, fighting against Thee and calling Thine Apostle a liar. O Allah, destroy them!'

Two Meccan chiefs, Shaiba and Otha, with Otha's son Waleed, stepped forward in bold challenge. Three Medina warriors promptly faced them but Muhammad ordered them back and called on his own clan, the Beni Hashim men, to fight. This drew forth Hamza, the Prophet's uncle, and his cousins Ali ibn abi Talid and Ubaida ibn Harith. Two of the Muslim champions won their duels while the third was wounded and soon bled to death. The preliminaries over, the tribes met in wild and bloody combat. As the fighting raged Muhammad became distraught and repeatedly prayed wildly to Allah, seeking his intervention. Watching the battle and fearful of the outcome, he shouted his great promise, 'All who die today will go to Paradise!'

According to the Muslim story, a young man

who had been standing beside the Prophet eating dates, now cried, 'What, is it only necessary to be killed by these people to enter Paradise!' Sword in hand, he charged into the massed Kuraish warriors and cut down several before he collapsed from his own wounds. Such wild valour, inspired by Muhammad's prayers and promises, forced the Kuraish back, and soon they broke and ran. Among the 50 enemy dead was Abu Jahal, a bitter enemy of Muhammad, who sent a servant to find the corpse; this man cut off and brought back Jahal's head. 'The head of the enemy of God!' Muhammad cried. 'Praise God, for there is no God but he!'

Some Muslims wanted to massacre the 50 or so prisoners but pragmatism triumphed over vengeance; it made more sense to hold the captives for ransom. Modern equivalents of this thinking are the cases of the American hostages held in Iran 1979–80 and of those held by Shi'a fanatics in Lebanon in 1985–88. Islam has long realized that dead men have no value.

The *Koran* proclaimed that the horde of Meccan unbelievers at Badr had been routed by Allah himself. The victory was compared in magnitude with the escape of the Israelites from Pharaoh. A Muslim who could say 'I fought at Badr' was treated with profound respect and Muhammad's prestige grew enormously. So did the acceptance of jihad, after its first battle. This holy war had worked. The psychological victory was immense and uncommitted tribes now joined Muhammad. As so often in

Islamic military history, the undecided masses joined the winner.

Muhammad exploited his advantage by attacking his main Jewish critics, the Kainuka, who lived in a fortified part of Medina. After a 15-day siege they surrendered and were driven into exile, all their property being looted by the Muslims. Jihad, they now felt, had justified itself.

After Muhammad's death Muslim armies, inspired by the spirit of jihad, went on to conquer much of the then known world. In many cases a subjugated people themselves became Muslim and joined the great march of Islam throughout Arabia, much of Asia and virtually all the Mediterranean.

Islamic pressure was relentless and victories came swiftly. Having taken much of Spain, in 732 a Muslim army penetrated deep into France to be stopped at Tours, then beaten and forced back in one of the most decisive battles of history. In Spain Muslims fought Christians for eight centuries; not until the siege and capture of Granada in 1492 was the Muslim hold broken. Other Muslim armies battered at the gates of eastern Europe for centuries and several times came close to capturing Vienna. But the zest for holy war was unabated even in defeat.

CHAPTER FOUR

Conquest for Allah

Jihad is a passionately held ideal and Islam's most dominant obsession. As already explained the word means literally 'extraordinary effort' or great striving for Allah. Because this effort is nowhere more strenuous than in war, jihad came to mean holy war. Its aim is direct – the subjection of unbelievers to Islam. In modern times other means and ends have been attached to holy war but the fundamental principle of conquest in the name of Allah is constant. Together the passion for action and the principle of Islamic domination have made jihad difficult for Western Christians to comprehend.

Yet the rules and concepts of holy war have remained constant for centuries. They are virtually *unchangeable* because they were laid down in the *Koran*, reinforced by the Hadith (the traditional sayings and actions of Muhammad), endorsed by the Shari'a (the law of Islam) and confirmed by Fikq (the science of jurisprudence in Islam).

Differences exist in the application of jihad, according to the four main Schools of Islamic law, but these differences are in the superstructure of jihad, not in its solid base. Some of Islam's commands and promises are still powerful after thirteen centuries, such as the effect of the promise of

Paradise for those who fight in the cause of holy war.

At Medina Muhammad himself had divided all men and all communities into just two groups – Dar al-Islam, the lands of Islam, and Dar al-Harb, the lands of war. Writing in 1978 the great Pakistani Muslim scholar Allah Bukhsh K. Brohl, notes[1] that 'Islam views the world as though it were bipolarized in two opposing camps – Dar al-Islam facing Dar al-Harb. The first one is submissive to Allah in co-operating with his purpose to establish peace, order and other such pre-conditions of human development, but the second one, on the other hand, is engaged in perpetuating defiance of the same Allah.'

Also, Muhammad's simple preaching formula – 'There are no gods but one God' – is as effective now as it was in the seventh century. In the first Islamic century it cut across all tribal bounds and achieved complete unity of the faithful. The Muslim battle-cry of 'Allahu Akbar!' – 'God is great!' – expresses both unity and fervour. It was used by Muhammad's own warriors – and more than thirteen centuries later by the Iranian soldiers who stormed Iraqi positions in the Gulf War. Significantly the battle-cry of Palestinian and Syrian Muslims fighting the Christian Lebanese in Beirut in the period 1976–1982 was 'Din al Islam aqwa!' – 'The faith of Islam is stronger!'

Many Muslim Arabs say that the military suc-

---

[1] In a preface to *The Quranic Concept of War*, Lahore.

cesses which brought about the spread of Islam across the world were ordained by Allah and revealed in advance to the Prophet Muhammad. Since this was so, they argue, the true world religion, Islam, was dynamic and fully in force from the moment of its revelation. It did not have to develop or evolve. No wonder then that Muslims believe that Islam is stronger than Christianity, Judaism, Hinduism, Buddhism and all other 'misconceived' religions.

The idea of holy war had been born out of Muhammad's necessity to make the infant Islam strong. After his time it was nourished by sheer aggression, banner-waving pride, Islamic confidence and a total sense of righteousness of cause. It took on a force which led to its astonishing expansion. No other religion (though Islam is a complete way of life, not only a religion) has ever inspired so many men so consistently and so eagerly to be heedless of death and of the dangers of battle. Jihadic warriors were fanatically courageous and ferociously single-minded. In modern times the discipline of armies has not diluted but directed this fanaticism.

Such devotion to the Islamic cause should not be underestimated – though it often is. Muhammad had insisted that his followers abandon all family ties; he told them that the only relatives of a believer were his brother Muslims. Fear of shedding the blood of fellow tribesmen had no relevance to Muhammad's Muslims and several are said to have killed their own unbelieving fathers or

brothers. Apart from this, many of the Prophet's
men were destitute – having abandoned all their
property in Mecca when they left it to follow
Muhammad – and therefore they were desperate.
Their only asset was their sword. To desperation
and fanaticism was added a form of discipline,
brought about by Muhammad's policy of prayer
five times a day. The men lined up parade-fashion
and went through the motions and words of prayer
in unison, as their leader directed. Their enemies
have rarely had comparable psychological advantages to boost morale.

Some Islamic scholars say that the Western mind
has been too influenced by centuries of dramatic
and blood-curdling stories of scimitar-wielding
Muslims – Turks, Persians, Moors, Berbers and
Arabs generally – charging into battle against their
Christian enemies. Led by the green, black or red
banners of Islam and shouting invocations to Allah,
these warriors have been unfairly accused of atrocities, Islam's defenders claim. The stories, over-
coloured though many of them might be, are
nevertheless based on countless real raids, battles
and wars. In more reasoned accounts, highly
regarded historians confirm that the melodramatic
fiction has a solid base in truth. By underestimating
Islam's vehemence and violence Islam's apologists
denigrate its sincerity and strength.

It would be easy to get the impression that
Arabia before Islam was peaceful. In fact, for
countless centuries warfare was waged regularly for
a certain period each year as an ordinary part of the

routine of tribal life and it was as natural as birth and death. One motive was the desire for plunder; in that harsh and arid terrain raiding was an economic necessity, a matter of survival. Another motive was revenge for a killing, perhaps incurred in an earlier raid; the blood feud cycle of killing – revenge-killing – killing was endless. Equally important, war was a relief from the monotony of desert existence.

Again, young men needed to prove themselves to the older men while the older men felt obliged to give a lead, as fighting men, to the younger ones. Some tribes lived for generations in a state of conflict for reasons which no longer had any meaning – yet neither tribe wanted to end it. Battles were sometimes arranged on an annual basis – as those between the Kuraish and the Hawazin tribes. An appointment would be made and the warriors turned up and violently attacked each other until they felt that enough men had been killed or maimed.

The coming of Islam added a new motive to war which channelled violence into more deliberate and systematic warlike activities. But even in Islam's early years jihad was not limited to open war. It was all forms of fighting, aggression and conflict provided they could be justified as 'holy'. More frequently, aggression was rationalized rather than justified; what the *Koran* states or is interpreted as having stated is so absolute that justification is meaningless and irrelevant. Consequently, even murder and assassination have been part of holy war throughout Islam's history.

Some orientalists and 'Arabists' equate jihad with 'the spread of Islam' by arms. While accurate, this is too simplistic, especially in the late 20th century when Islam is also being spread by propaganda and economic pressure.

Jihad quickly reached its important position in Islamic thought and practice. The chapters of the *Koran* revealed to Muhammad in Mecca (610–622) taught patience under attack. Muslims, being then in the minority, had no option but to be patient. In the chapters he produced at Medina (after 622) the right to repel attack became dominant. Gradually this grew into a prescribed duty of the Muslims of Medina to take the initiative and fight to subdue the hostile people of Mecca. Thus holy war had its origin in the vital need of Muhammad to establish his authority. We cannot be certain that Muhammad realized that the position he was taking up implied constant and unprovoked war against the unbelieving world until it submitted to Islam. He certainly had a universal Islam in his mind, as the stories of his letters and messages to the surrounding tribes indicate.

'I have been ordered to fight the people,' Muhammad said, 'until they profess that there is no God but Allah and that Muhammad is his messenger, until they perform the salak (the ritual prayers) and pay the zakat (the alms tax). If they do so their life and property are safe from me, except in cases where the law of Islam permits it to be taken and they are then responsible before Allah.'

Koranic passages speak many times of the unbelievers who must be subdued, as they are 'dangerous' or 'faithless.' Dangerous they might have been but to ascribe faithlessness to them is illogical as they had their own faith or they were pagan. They could not be 'faithless' apostates; as they had not yet embraced Islam they could hardly renounce it.

Traditions (Hadith) about jihad are as important as *Koranic* injunctions. For instance, 'The man who dies without having taken part in a raid or without having made the decision to do so, dies a hypocrite.' This reduces jihad to the individual level, to the personal obligation.

Soon jihad became a *fard ala'l-kifaya* – a duty imposed on all male, adult and free Muslims, sane in mind and having the means to reach the Muslim army assembling for holy war. The qualifications about sanity and ability to travel had little meaning since not joining the army was considered in itself a form of insanity and a Muslim male was expected to go to any lengths and to suffer any privation to enlist in a jihad. Jihad nearly became the sixth *rukn* or fundamental duty of Muslims and is regarded as such by descendants of the Kharidjis, the members of the earliest of the religious sects of Islam.

A fundamental tenet of jihad concerns the Islamic belief that sovereignty lies in God rather than in the people; it then becomes logical that rebellion against the state is viewed not merely as an act of civil disobedience but also as an infringement of the will of Allah. Taken a step further, it is the manifest will of Allah that all men subscribe to Islam; those who do not are obviously enemies of Allah.

The duty to fight, Islamic tradition insists, is continuous until the whole world is under the rule of Islam and it must be controlled or headed by a Muslim imam or leader. Until recent times it was considered, in theory at least, that the Shi'a Muslims could not have a jihad until their 'invisible' imam reappeared. The principal stronghold of Shi'a Islam is Iran and many Iranians from 1979 on regarded Ayatollah Khomeini as the missing imam.

Wars against unbelievers were always not only *right* in the religious sense, they were right as law. The Shari'a required a Muslim head of state to organize a raid into enemy territory once a year as a legal ritual to remind everybody, including the Muslims themselves, of Islamic obligations. Even in times of peace Muslims were expected to undergo military training and prepare their weapons and material for the inevitable jihad to come. But as so often in Islamic practice a ruler had a way out of his holy war duties.

Some later Islamic jurists said that a ruler could fulfil his obligations just by making annual preparations for jihad, even if he did not then go to war. But often enough the preparations generated so much warlike momentum that conflict became almost inevitable. For many centuries men brought together as an army looked forward to war as a means of gaining loot, women and slaves; a ruler who assembled a force and then disbanded it without going to war ran the risk of the men turning against him.

Once holy war had been proclaimed against a particular people they were given the opportunity, by *Koranic* edict, to embrace Islam though the period for reflection was sometimes very short. Should they refuse to convert they were given another chance – this time to accept Muslim rule and become *dhimmis* (second-class citizens) and to pay *djizya* (tribute or poll-tax) and *kharadj* (tax paid on land). If they rejected this offer the only option left was to fight. As losers they would be enslaved, men, women and children, and all their property would be booty; four-fifths of it was divided among the conquering soldiers, one-fifth went to their leader.

Muslims regarded the choices given to non-Muslims as fair. Even when the armies were on the battlefield, face to face, the unbelievers could embrace Islam and save themselves. Muslims regarded this as a generous concession; the people about to be attacked would from that moment become part of the Muslim community, entitled to its rights and bound to its duties. Those who converted to Islam to save their lives and then switched back to their former faith were regarded as apostates and put to death. It was a definite duty of Muslims to show hostility towards pagans, when encountered. Many Arab slave-traders later used this teaching as a rationalization for rounding up negroes in Africa.

The situation of a Muslim country invaded by unbelievers – as with the British and French empire-builders in Africa and Asia for instance – was different from that of an Islamic state setting forth on holy war. The leader could issue a general summons calling all Muslims living there, whether nationals of the country or not, to take up arms.

Now, as then, as the danger grows so does the scope of the summons until the entire Muslim world is involved. In the Arab–Israeli war of 1948, again in 1973 and 1979–82 general calls to jihad were made, though not necessarily universally heeded.

In a strong sense *all* Muslim wars are holy wars; even when Muslims fight Muslims both sides invoke the name of Allah. In 1980 Iraq and Iran, engaged in bloody battle for mastery of the Persian (or Arabian) Gulf, proclaimed jihad against the other. It has always been easy for Sunni and Shi'a nations and groups or any of the many sects of Islam to accuse another of 'crimes against Allah.' The judicial murder in Iran of 100,000 'enemies of the state' between 1979 and 1987 was actually sanctioned by Muhammad at Medina, according to the judges of the Revolutionary Courts.

Throughout history, when Muslims won their battle against unbelievers those enemy fighters who survived the fighting could not expect their lives to be spared merely because they were prisoners; there is no such provision under Islamic law.

Again, they had the option: Convert to Islam or accept the *dhimmi* second-class citizen contract or die. This was often not clearly explained to prisoners, many of whom expected to be spared by the customs to which they themselves subscribed. It is reasonable to suppose that tens of thousands would have become Muslims had they realized this would save their lives.

Another aspect of Islamic law led to countless executions. Should a Muslim leader promise to spare the lives of an entire town or fort he makes a contract for himself alone; another leader superseding him is not bound to continue the arrangement. This explains some of the apparent betrayals of trust so frequently mentioned in the history of warfare between Muslims and others when captured people who had been promised their lives were later massacred.

Some Schools of Law claim that not all unbeliever prisoners or occupied peoples are entitled to *dhimmi* status; and that only Christians, Jews and Zoroastrians are so privileged, as the 'people of the book' – the Old or New Testaments. Other unbelievers have the straight choice of embracing Islam or being slain.

The classical doctrine of jihad was militant and it remains so. The notion that its militancy has declined may be the result of the fact that Islamic governments issue fewer formal declarations of jihad, therefore jihad is less obvious. There is much reference to *defensive* and *offensive* jihad. To fundamentalists these distinctions are meaningless because jihad is universal, timeless, endless and revolutionary. It is essentially aggressive and so total that to classify or qualify it in any way makes no sense. All that has changed in modern times is that the 'submission' required of unbelievers has been broadened. It is impractical for citizens of the United States, Britain or France or other non-Muslim countries to become *dhimmis* in the accepted sense but they can secure protected status by implicit or explicit acceptance of Islamic over-lordship. Implicit acceptance could be dependence on Muslim oil or money; explicit acceptance could be practical aid given to Muslim states, especially in the military sense, or approval of political attitudes.

Much written by Khomeini and other Muslim jurists and thinkers explains the remorseless thrust of holy war. The Sunni Muslim Code of Civil Legislation according to the Hanifi school of Islamic Law expresses the matter clearly. The jihad is the normal and permanent state of war between Muslims and the people of Dar al-Harb, the Code points out. It can end only with domination over the unbelievers and the absolute supremacy of Islam throughout the world. All warlike acts are permitted on the territory of the infidels.

As it is not feasible to fight against all the infidel peoples (*harbis*) simultaneously, jihad allows for the eventuality of a provisional suspension of hostilities. Such unavoidable truces constitute another form of holy war for they serve to reinforce the military potential of Dar al-Islam.

A great modern Islamic scholar, Dr Muhammad Hamidullah, explains to Muslims how Muhammad himself approached the problem of conquest.

The Prophet Muhammad always preferred, both as a general policy and a point of principle, to overwhelm the enemy but not to annihilate him. The means were twofold: Bringing economic pressure to bear and ceaselessly increasing his own military might with a long-range policy. He struck at the right moment when the enemy would not dare offer any resistance and his objective could be reached in a bloodless manner. The resources and energies of the enemy, preserved intact, and redirected in better and constructive channels, could but add to the power of the Islamic State.

While the jurists, the scholars and the theologians can readily explain many abstract aspects of jihad, none of these aspects makes comprehensible to the Western mind the commitment of the individual Muslim to holy war. Only the promise of Paradise can do that. (See Chapter Six.)

CHAPTER FIVE

War according to the Koran

With the upsurge of Islamic interest in jihad and with increasing numbers of militants becoming dedicated to it much is being written by Muslims about the subject. Scholars, journalists and prominent soldiers within Islam are studying it and writing about it from their various viewpoints.

For the non-Muslim people of Dar al-Harb – who are the 'targets' of jihad – probably no book is more revealing than *The Quranic[1] Concept of War* by the Pakistani Brigadier S.K. Malik, published in 1979.

That a holy book, of all books, can provide a concept of war is interesting but not surprising. Islamic military history lists 81 campaigns which Muhammad fought in Arabia in the 10-year period, AD 622–632 They fall naturally into these time-scale groups:

Pre-Badr raids and liaison missions
Operations between Badr and Ohad
Campaigns between Ohad and Khandaq
Campaigns between Khandaq and Khyber
Campaigns between Khyber and Mecca
Campaigns between Mecca and Doma

[1] This is one of several transliterations for the name of the Islamic holy book. I use *Koranic* which is more usual in the West.

As Muhammad had such an impressive military background it is natural that the *Koran* is taken so seriously as the basis for a training manual.

It is commonplace in Islamic military academies for instructors to use Muhammad's major battles as case studies from which to draw political, military and ethical lessons. The battles most commonly dealt with in this way are those of Badr 624, Ohad 625, the siege of Medina 627, Muta 629, Mecca 630, Hunain 630 and the expedition to Tabuk 630. Malik's textbook runs to 158 pages and is required reading in many Islamic military colleges. President Zia al-Huq, who was then Pakistan's Chief of the Army Staff, wrote a foreword for Malik's work in which he said, 'This book brings out with simplicity, clarity and precision the Quranic philosophy on the application of military force, within the context of the totality that is Jihad. The professional soldier in a Muslim army, pursuing the goals of a Muslim state, CANNOT [Zia's emphasis] become professional if in all his activities he does not take on "the colour of Allah . . ."'

The author himself says that his book is necessary to 'lay bare those secrets of war which the human mind has been struggling to decipher for ages. It should be undertaken to obtain a total and overall view of the divine theories and concepts of war.' The *Koranic* philosophy of war, Malik states, is 'infinitely supreme and effective.'

The military campaigns undertaken or initiated by the Prophet Muhammad are institutions for learning the Koranic art of war, Malik tells his

readers. Some of Muhammad's experiences show
that a small force can, by intelligent use of its geo-
political and geo-strategical position, adopt tactics
superior to those of its more powerful adversaries.

Malik does not enlarge on this point but Muslims
who study his book assume that he refers to
Muslims exploiting their natural advantages. For
instance, the militant Iranian and Lebanese Shi'as,
though numerically and militarily weak compared
with the American armed forces, inflicted a defeat
upon them in Beirut in 1983 and forced the United
States government to order a military withdrawal.
This victory was accomplished by using 'natural'
political and strategical advantages. The Shi'as
knew that the US would not, for political reasons,
make a full-scale invasion of Lebanon. Also, the
Shi'as and their Syrian allies held such a strategi-
cally strong position that the American battleship
New Jersey fired one-ton shells into enemy positions without causing any significant damage.

Commenting that the *Koranic* philosophy of war
is immensely rich in its moral and humanitarian
contents, Malik promises that under ideal conditions jihad can produce a direct result and 'force
its will upon the enemy.' Over and over he stresses
the value of terror, which should preferably be
used during the preparatory stages of war. If this
chance is missed, then terror should be applied
during the actual fighting. At the same time Muslims must be able to withstand any efforts the
enemy might make to strike terror into them. Their
own Faith must therefore be strong.

He covers his subject comprehensively under these chapter headings: Historical Perspective; The Causes of War; The Ethics of War; The Strategy of War; The Conduct of War; The Application of Quranic Military Thought. Finally, he makes a summary of major conclusions.

Some of Malik's assertions – the *Koran* naturally leaves no room for argument so assertion is inevitable – throw clear light on the various aspects of the holy war now being fought on several 'fronts' against those whom Islam declares to be its enemies.

On the ethics of war, Malik states: 'In Islam a war is fought for the cause of Allah. A Muslim's cause of war is just, noble, righteous and humanitarian . . . Humanitarianism lies at the very heart of Islamic approach to war.'

Considering the frequent murder of prisoners and mutilation of corpses by holy war fighters this assertion seems strange. Nevertheless, the *Koran* does say that once the enemy has been 'subdued' and prisoners are taken they should be treated humanely, the choice being only between 'generosity and ransom.' The precedent is that at the battle of Hunain in 630 the Muslims captured a large number of prisoners; all of them were repatriated on the payment of ransom. The ransom of some of them, who were too poor to pay it, was said to have been paid personally by Muhammad. There is wide divergence between the principle and practice of humanitarianism in jihad. For instance, Iraq used poison gas against Iranian soldiers but it still considers its cause to be 'just, noble and righteous.' The Iranian régime, having tortured to death many opponents within Iran, still claims to be humanitarian.

On strategy, Malik states, 'Terror struck into the hearts of the enemies is not only a means, it is the end in itself. Once a condition of terror into the opponent's heart is obtained hardly anything is left to be achieved. It is the point where the means and the end meet and merge. Terror is not a means of imposing decision upon the enemy; it is *the decision* we wish to impose upon him . . .'

This is one of the most significant observations in Malik's book and the various Muslim terror organizations in their actions against the Americans and others illustrate the principle which Malik deduces from the *Koran*. Terror was the foundation policy and tactic of the various factions which make up the Palestine Liberation Organization. Attacks on soft targets, such as schools, settlements, public buses and hotels, are meant to create terror. Malik would have many historical precedents for his statement that terror is the end in itself; they go back to the days of the first Muslim imperialists and to the original Assassins, who were active in Syria in the 12th century.

Malik is able to quote many passages from the *Koran* to support his own statements. These are a few of them from Chapter 8, *The Spoils*:

- When you meet an opposing army stand firm and pray fervently to Allah that you may triumph.

- Let not Unbelievers think that they can get away from us, the Godly (i.e. Muslims). Muster against them all the men at your disposal so that you may strike terror into the enemies of Allah.
- Whatever you spend in the cause of Allah shall be repaid to you and you will not be treated unjustly.
- Prophet, rouse the Believers to arms. If there are twenty among you, who are steadfast and persevering, they will vanquish two hundred; if a hundred, they will vanquish a thousand of the Unbelievers. Allah is with those that are steadfast.
- It is not you who slays the enemy, it is Allah.

From the chapter *The Imrans*, Malik quotes:

- And if you are slain or die in the cause of Allah forgiveness and mercy are far better than all you could amass in life. And if you die or are slain it is unto Allah that you are brought together.
- Soon we shall cast terror into the hearts of the Unbelievers . . . their abode will be fire; and evil is the home of the wrongdoers.

From Chapter 9, *Repentance*:

- Allah has purchased from the Believers their lives and their worldly goods and in return he has promised the Garden of Paradise; they will fight in His cause and slay and are slain. This promise is binding . . . and who is more faithful to his promise than Allah? Then rejoice in the bargain which you made; that is the supreme accomplishment.

The principles implicit in all these passages appear over and over in modern jihad's many guises, military, economic or religious.

Malik could have made even more use of *Koranic* passages to justify war. Many Muslim scholars refer to a passage from *Repentance*:

When the sacred months[2] are over slay the idolaters wherever you find them. Arrest them, besiege them, and lie in ambush everywhere for them.

Reference to conflict in the prohibited months occurs also in Chapter 2, *The Cow*:

They question you about fighting in the sacred months. Say to them, 'Fighting at this time is a grave offence but it is more serious in the sight of Allah to debar others from the path of Allah, to deny His existence and to expel his worshippers from the Sacred Mosque. Idolatry is worse than slaughter. (This last sentence appears twice.)

The passage appears in the *Koran* to justify Muhammad for having himself waged war in a sacred month; this action had caused criticism. The passage as a whole is taken to mean that even in a sacred month killing is preferable to allowing idolaters and enemies to stay at large.

Other *Koranic* passages which are instructive about war include these three from *The Spoils*:

● Prepare any military force you can muster against the enemy and any cavalry with which you can overawe Allah's enemy and your own enemy, as

[2] The sacred months, when warfare was prohibited, were Shawal, Dhul-Qa'aba, Dhul-Hajja, Muharram.

well as others besides them whom you do not know.

- A Prophet may not take captives until he has fought and triumphed in his land.
- Make war on the Unbelievers until idolatry is no more and Allah's religion is supreme.

And these passages:

- Whenever two factions of believers fall out with one another, then try to reconcile them. If one of them should oppress the other, then fight against the one who acts oppressively until they comply with God's command. If they comply, then set things right again between them in all justice. Chapter 49, *The Chambers*.
- You who believe, do not make friends with anyone other than your own people. They will continually cause you trouble and they like to do anything that will distress you. Chapter 3, *The Imrans*.
- The penalty for those who wage war on Allah and his messenger and spread havoc through the land, is to be slaughtered or crucified, or to have their hands and feet cut off on opposite sides, or to be banished from the land. Chapter 5, *The Table*.
- Attack anyone who attacks you to the same extent as he attacked you.
- Fighting is obligatory for you, much as you dislike it . . . Both from Chapter 2, *The Cow*.

In his summary, Malik tells his readers that the *Koran* does not visualize war being waged with kid gloves. It wants the nation and the individual to be at war 'in toto, that is, with all their spiritual, moral and physical resources.' And, he says, Muslims must wage war with 'all our person, goods, might and main.'

The modern scholar Abdullah Yusuj Ali, author of one of the most famous commentaries on the *Koran*, concurs with Malik and says of holy war:

Let us be under no illusion about jihad. If we are not prepared to fight for our faith, with our lives and all our resources, both our lives and our resources will be wiped out by our enemies. As to life, Allah gave it and a coward is not likely to save it.

Ali bases this interpretation on verse 243 of Chapter 11, Houd (the Prophet Houd).

Brigadier Malik, Dr Ali and others contrast traditional thinking on war with *Koranic* thinking. Malik, in fact, takes a statement from an American student of strategy, Edward Meade Earle, and uses it as a key for contrast. Earle, in his book *The Makers of Modern Strategy* (Princeton University Press, London, 1952), says: 'War is not an act of God. It grows out of what people, statesmen and nations do or do not do.'

Malik says: 'The Quranic view on war is quite different . . . the very initiation of war is for the cause of God. It is, therefore, controlled and conditioned by the "Word of God" [that is, as expressed in the *Koran*] from its inception till culmination.'

It is this conviction that war *is* an act of God and an act *for* God which makes Islamic holy war so formidable. It is not possible to engage in intellectual argument with Muslims about what people in the Christian West might consider the excesses of holy war because they cannot recognize excess. And it is difficult to find a way of combating a form of warfare whose warriors feel themselves to be invincible because they are doing God's work. In the cause of Allah, Muslims do not merely have His permission to fight but His *command* to fight.

CHAPTER SIX

Love of martyrdom, certainty of Paradise

In May 1982 an Austrian journalist was permitted to visit the southern part of the Iraq–Iran battle-front near Khorramshahr and became one of the few foreign spectators to witness a bizarre military event.

Heavy artillery of both armies was thundering across the battlefield and aircraft were fighting each other and making rocket-attack runs against the guns but in the region visible to the journalist nothing much seemed to be happening. Hundreds of Iranian tanks, with their engines idling, were hidden in the rough country on the Iranian side of the battlefield. Some distance behind them were truck-loads of infantry and other soldiers in armoured personnel carriers. The Austrian, with the few other foreign observers, anticipated an Iranian attack but it did not appear imminent.

Surprisingly, scores of ordinary civilian single-decker buses, with some grey-painted army buses, arrived behind the low dunes and hills and dis-gorged thousands of boys. Some appeared to be no older than ten while others were teenagers. They wore ordinary clothes but tied around their heads were black cloths like handkerchiefs and around each neck was a metal tag. The cloths were martyrs' frontlets with a text in Persian which read *One who will love martyrdom.*

The watching foreigners saw that large numbers of the younger boys were roped together in groups of about twenty. Noisy and excited, they were shouting slogans praising Khomeini and the revolution interspersed with others damning Saddam Hussein, president of Iraq, and similar evil-doers.

Uniformed officers, both from the Iranian regular army and the Pasdaran or Revolutionary Guards, marshalled the boys into long ranks and moved them forward, up the gentle slopes and down towards the flat land where the actual front line was situated.

When whistles were blown the boys ran forward in lines which were kept more or less straight and even by the ropes which joined them. They looked, to the Austrian, 'like children racing down a beach to enter the water for a swim.' He noticed that the men did not go forward with the boys but stayed well back, with automatic rifles cradled in their arms.

When one wave of boys had run about fifty metres forward another wave was sent after them and all the time they shouted. According to the reporter, none of his group understood the purpose of the rush until the first mine exploded. In fact, the boys were running into Iraqi minefields which blocked what would otherwise be an easy route of approach for the Iranian tanks.

Many of the boys were blown to pieces. The shocked Austrian saw gaps suddenly appear in the

lines and rope-ends tied around forearms which
suddenly had no body attached to them. Along a
front of something like four or five kilometres
waves of boys were 'clearing' the minefields by
blowing up the mines with their bodies.

Even with ghastly slaughter in front of them the
second wave – and in some places, a third wave –
did not falter but ran into almost certain death.
The mine clearance operation lasted perhaps ten
minutes and by that time the ground was littered
with corpses. Some wounded boys dragged themselves out of the area; others tried to do so but
couldn't because of the ropes which anchored them
to a dead comrade. Others were standing, apparently on the other side of the minefield, after
having run several hundred metres.

Then the tanks revved up, the armoured personnel carriers moved up close behind them and the
real attack went forward through the openings
made by the boys. Some of them, living and dead,
were crushed under the tanks' tracks.

There was a certain macabre logic in the Iranian
leaders' tactics of using the volunteer suicide warriors; Iran was short of tanks but manpower – or
boypower – was plentiful. According to official
communiqués, the Iranian army made good progress that day. They paid a tribute to the *basseej*
units.

The *Basseej* are the young martyrs. At that time
most parents willingly surrendered their sons for
Khomeini's use in holy war. They knew, as the
boys did, that the metal tag around their necks was
a key to Paradise. Youths would tell foreign visi-

tors, 'I would love to become a martyr for Khomeini. Allah has bestowed this blessing on my friends and my blessing will come.'

The parents also had a blessing, not only in their sons' martyrdom but in the Martyrs' Certificates they received from the government. Many mothers carry with them large photographs of their dead sons, though, apparently with rare exceptions, they do not complain. As mothers of martyrs they have a higher social status than others.

Martyrdom has solid advantages. The so-called Martyrs' Fund has developed into an economic factor of imposing size, supported by the State treasury, nationalized industries and private donations. From this fund martyrs' families derive privileges not given to other members of the community – cash payments, free access to otherwise rationed daily requirements and sought-after consumer goods.

Propaganda films about martyrdom are commonplace. I saw one in Lebanon which depicts a mother in the main story line, backed by sequences from the front or from other places where Islamic heroes are waging war. The mother rages against the cowards who run away and laments when she has to dig her own son's grave. Nevertheless she realizes that it was only right that he should die for his fatherland.

When the fighting is severe the names and portraits of the martyrs fill the newspaper pages, column after column of them. Each obituary concludes by describing their final deed of valour.

Ayatollah Khomeini said of a 17-year-old volunteer who threw himself under an Iraqi tank with a belt of explosives around his waist, 'These children are the nation's leaders.'

A common slogan of the would-be martyrs is *Marg bat Amrika* – Death to America – death to all foreign powers who in one big satanic conspiracy are preventing the spreading of the true faith.

For Muslims, especially those of the Shi'a faction, martyrdom is holy war's reward. The martyr is assured of Paradise – and Paradise is infinitely desirable. So desirable, as Hussein Moussawi had told me, that a man going to certain death can smile.

Muhammad, a town Arab, grew up in the burning heat of a valley so it was natural that he should conceive Paradise as on a cool mountain-top and so present it in the *Koran*. A spring is constantly bubbling and around it are comfortable chairs on brightly coloured carpets. Here the chosen people loll in green satin garments with silver buckles while they drink the spring water mixed with expensive spices or exquisite wine from jugs which give off a musky perfume. Fruit and grapes are there for the plucking. The open square of Paradise is surrounded by trees which give that most blessed of desert benefits, shade. Most important of all, the men who reach this refuge enjoy the carnal company of dark-eyed virgins (houris) to whom Allah has granted eternal youth. While these joys are specially calculated for men some women may also expect entry to Paradise; they are promised Allah's greeting, joy, and freedom from hatred and envy. The unworthy and the infidels are promised fire where they will forever abide without relief; when they want a drink they will get only boiling water.

Islamic narratives abound with reference to the profound and passionate wish of the early Muslims to reach this Paradise as soon as possible. A martyr's death was actively sought. General Sir John Glubb, who spent much of his life commanding Arab soldiers, believes that the promise of Paradise was perhaps the most powerful factor in promoting the great Arab conquests of past centuries.

When Islam's conquering years seemed to be over, martyrdom lost its attraction. In the latter part of the twentieth century it is again a goal and a reward. The Shi'a obsession with martyrdom is greater than that of the larger Sunni branch of Islam. The word Shi'a means partisan; Shi'as are partisans or followers of Ali, who, they say, was designated by Muhammad as his successor; Ali was Muhammad's cousin and son-in-law. Instead, the succession went to a progression of caliphs.

Some distinctions between Shi'ism and Sunnism are more profound than a dispute over succession. Shi'ism has unique characteristics that affect the political as well as the religious behaviour of its adherents. The violent deaths of Ali and his son Hussein instilled in the Shi'as an admiration and desire for martyrdom. They claim to be closer to the precepts of the *Koran* than the Sunnis are. During the sacred month of Muharram they became highly charged religiously and emotionally

and martyrdom at this time becomes almost com-
pulsive. Muharram is indeed the martyrdom
season and it was during this season that the 1983
attacks on the American and French bases in Beirut
were made.

Ayatollah Khomeini and other Iranian ayatollahs
as well as Islamic theologians make great play of
Paradise as the glorious prize for those Muslims
who become martyrs in Allah's name.

The Iranians have promoted the appeal of Paradise in a wide-ranging way – in their internal
propaganda about the war against Iraq, in their
campaign of vilification against the Arab monarchies and against Israel, in the continuous push of
the Islamic revolution, and in their exploitation of
the people of southern Lebanon.

Many religious leaders in speeches and in posters and pamphlets have stressed the certainty of
instant Paradise for those who die while killing
infidels. Iranian priests of various rank (strictly
speaking Islam has no ordained clergy) have been
posted to Lebanon, Saudi Arabia and many other
places and one of their main missions is to spread
the good news about Paradise.

Many events have proved their success. One of
their greatest triumphs was to induce women and
girls to become suicide attackers. One, Sana Mhay-
dali, became known as the 'Queen' (or 'Bride') of
'the South' – that is, of southern Lebanon. That she
and others were so completely indoctrinated with
the promise of Paradise is interesting because while
the *Koran* does not exclude women from Paradise

it does not specifically welcome them to it. The holy book's phraseology throughout gives the strong impression that Paradise is mainly for men – other than the virgins whose company they are to enjoy.

Thanks to a propaganda video tape which Sana recorded before her martyr's mission, she became an instant celebrity but the details of her background have not previously been published. I found out a good deal about her in the summer of 1985 when I was travelling in southern Lebanon. Born at Unkun in the Saida district, Sana was the daughter of a customs officer and the youngest of a family of four. She finished her school studies in 1982, at the age of 14, and started work in a video shop near her home.

She met many young people in this shop including a boy by whom she became pregnant. Pregnancy for an Arab girl is disastrous; her family considers itself dishonoured and the offending girl might well be killed by her father, brothers, uncles or some other male relative. Any punishment for the killer is nominal because society approves of his act. Sana, aware of the danger, left her home and her job, on 23 March 1985, and was picked up by the local agent of the Syrian Popular Party, Abd el-Trzi.

Trzi and his colleagues considered her to be a potential suicide attacker against the Israeli army. Her friends told me that they exploited her despair at being pregnant. 'Sana didn't really want to be a martyr,' I was told, 'but the men talked her into it.'

Trzi had another idea – to film Sana's 'holy mission' and to call her 'Bride of the South.' The plan was put to the Iranian mullahs in Baalbek, who approved it.

Sana could not drive so her recruiters gave her an elementary lesson in putting a car into gear and steering it. While the preparations were being made she was repeatedly assured that Paradise awaited her, despite her 'dishonour' at becoming pregnant. In fact, martyrdom was the only way she could wipe out that stain on the family's name.

One day in April 1985 the men rigged a car as a bomb and push-started it for Sana's last journey. She succeeded in ramming an Israeli military vehicle, killing two Israeli soldiers and herself. For a few days Sana was front-page news throughout the world.

The three-minute propaganda film made by the men who controlled her showed her neatly dressed in a two-piece suit and a red beret. Smiling throughout her monologue, Sana said:

I hope that my soul will embrace the spirits of those martyrs who preceded me . . . I hope that our souls will form an explosive mixture that will blow up as an earthquake on the heads of the enemy . . . I am very relaxed as I go to do this operation, which I have chosen because I am carrying out my duty to my people. I am from the group that decided on self sacrifice and martyrdom for the sake of the liberation of land and people . . .

Her friends told me that Trzi and the other men had introduced Sana to hashish – which is common in Lebanon – and to 'other drugs'. She had been given some kind of drug stimulant, they said, before she made the film and before she set off on her mission.

The Cyprus-published *Middle East Times* commented: 'What did Sana's Shi'a mentors tell her? Did they have no reservations in telling her that a fiery death in an exploding car was better than a life of friendship, family and love? Clearly they were happy to have such a beautiful martyr. But in this case the Shi'a use of religious images and promises of heaven is truly corrupt . . . The grim fact is that Sana was lured to her death by those older than herself whom she trusted, but who were willing to use her life for their own sake.'

This last comment is not quite true: Trzi, the mullahs and the others who were part of the conspiracy had nothing personal to gain by Sana's death. They used her in the name of holy war and it is quite certain that they had no reservations about it. There are no reservations in jihad, as all the Muslim authorities on the subject frequently point out.

Other Shi'a girls from Beirut and southern Lebanon, inspired by Sana's example and encouraged by announcements in the mosques that she was now in Paradise, volunteered for similar missions. I met one of them at a press conference in south Beirut. Her name was given as Muna and her age as 18. A little taller than average, and slim, she was an attractive girl, even though her hair was hidden by the headscarf she wore. The only word that can

do her expression justice is radiant. She glowed
with the pride of the dedicated, God-protected
martyr. She did not actually answer any questions
directly; all communication was through a man of
about 35 who translated her responses. It was clear
that she was not afraid, that she believed she was
going to Paradise, and the waiting for a suitable
mission was not unnerving her. She was completely
armoured by her faith as a 'soldier of Allah'; this
term was mentioned several times.

I do not know if Muna was later killed but several
girls have made suicide attacks. Some of them were
failures – the girls survived. These incidents are
described in another chapter.

Shi'a Muslim holy war terrorists are traditionally
more inspired by a longing for martyrdom than the
Muslims of the Sunni majority. This has been
changing as Shi'a agents set out to recruit Sunnis
for training as suicide attackers. Their success in
indoctrinating some Palestinians became evident
on 27 December 1985 when two killer squads
embarked on massacres at Vienna and Rome airports. With grenades and automatic rifles they
attacked passengers checking in at the counters of
the Israeli state airline, El Al. They killed 18
people of several different nationalities and
wounded another 118. The seven gunmen concerned were members of a group known as Martyrs
of Palestine. The organization is backed and
financed by Libya and the terrorists themselves
were trained in Iran. Travelling on Algerian and
Tunisian passports, supplied by sympathizers in

those countries, the terrorists reached their target countries via Syria and Lebanon.

Libya's official news agency, quoting President Gaddafi, praised the massacre as an 'heroic operation by Palestinian martyrs.' Similar comments were made publicly in Syria, Lebanon, Iraq and Algeria.[1]

Relevant *Koranic* references to martyrdom include:

- And say not of those who are slain in the way of Allah, 'They are dead.' Nay, they are living, though you do not perceive it. Chapter 2, verse 154.
- Think not of those who are slain in Allah's cause as dead. Nay, they live, finding their sustenance in the presence of their Lord. They rejoice in the bounty provided by Allah. And with regard to those left behind who have not yet joined them in their bliss, the Martyrs glory in the fact that on them is no fear, nor have they cause to grieve. Chapter 3, verses 170–171.

In one of the best known Islamic commentaries of the *Koran*, published by the Islamic Foundation, London, Abdullah Yussuf Ali says: 'This is a beautiful passage about the Martyrs in the cause of Truth. They are not dead; they live – and in a far higher and deeper sense than in the life they have left . . . The Martyrs not only rejoice at the bliss they have themselves attained; the dear ones left behind are in their thoughts. It is part of their glory

---

[1] See Chapter Fifteen for the Islamization of the PLO.

that they have saved their dear ones from fear, sorrow, humiliation and grief, in this life, even before they come to share in the glories of the Hereafter.

Those who leave their homes in the cause of Allah and are then slain or die . . . Allah will admit them to a place with which they will be well pleased, for Allah is all-knowing, most forbearing. Chapter 22, verses 58–59.

Yusuf Ali comments about this passage: 'Martyrdom is sacrifice in the service of Allah. Its reward is therefore greater than that of an ordinarily good life. The Martyr's sins are forgiven by the very act of martyrdom . . . Allah knows all his past life but will forbear from calling him to account for things that should strictly come into his account.'

Most Muslim terrorists undertake their designated missions in the conviction that Paradise awaits them should they be killed. The effect that this can have even on a man not brought up a Muslim was shown in the case of Ian Davidson, the Englishman who took part in the murder of three Israeli tourists at Larnaca, Cyprus, in 1985. During the court hearing and in interviews with journalists Davidson repeated over and over that he had 'never been happier' in his life than when murdering his victims for the PLO. This is the language of the Shi'a holy war fanatic who has killed for Allah.

CHAPTER SEVEN
High Command

The Western press has got into the habit of writing about 'shadowy' holy war warriors; similarly, there is a 'shadowy' Islamic Jihad Organization which has mysterious leaders. Speculation that the jihadic terrorist movement has no existence as a distinct group is wrong.

In fact, just as with any other army the Muslim holy war fighters have an organizational structure, with the equivalent of a general staff, sector commanders and others with special responsibilities, such as Intelligence and Special Operations, as well as paymasters, quartermasters and propaganda experts. Far from being shadowy, a good deal is known about the organization.

Islamic Jihad is made up of at least 30 terrorist bodies of Middle Eastern origin. It has an annual budget, with the money coming from Iran, Libya and Syria – though some groups might well have additional income from their own sources. The organization is governed by a council with five regional and several local commands.

The council calls itself the Supreme Co-ordinating Council and it co-ordinates the activities of two major groups; they are the Iranian Islamic Revolution and Islamic Revolutionary Organizations in the World. The Supreme Council is ruled from Iran by

Ayatollah Moussavi Khomeini and Ayatollah Hussein Ali Montazeri, though when he succeeds
Khomeini as the dictator of Iran – Khomeini has
named him as his heir – he may give up this post.
Members of the council include:

Muhsein Rafigh-Doust, Iranian minister for Revo-
lutionary Guards.
Muhammad Mir-Salim, Ayatollah Khomeini's
defence adviser.
Zabah Zankana, representative of Libya's secret
police in Teheran.
Mortada Chamran, representative of Lebanon's
Shi'a militia, Amal.
Hussein Moussavi, the Shi'a leader from Baalbek.
Ahmad Nahaullah, organizer of the Iranian under-
ground Shi'a cells in Saudi Arabia.

The head of Iran's national security service,
Muhammad Reyshari, is an adviser to the Co-
ordinating Council, though his principal work is
within Iran.

Five regional commands report to the Supreme
Council. They cover the Middle East, Iraq, United
States, Western Europe and Rest of World. This
last command has probably sub-divided into three
– South-east Asia and Australia; South America;
Africa.

The Middle East command HQ is at the Iranian
Embassy in Damascus and the leaders meet there
routinely twice a month. It has two leaders, Hussein Moussavi and Sheikh Fadlallah, who are cousins. Fadlallah is nominal chief and theological

adviser to the 'Hussein Suicide Commandos' but Moussavi is the operational head.

Moussavi tightly controls four main militant groups based in Lebanon. They are the 'Hussein Suicide Commandos,' the Defenders of the Islamic Revolution, the Revolutionary Amal Militia and Islamic Jihad. This group is quite separate from that of the organization as a whole; it is likely that some Western journalists, diplomats and intelligence agents have confused the two or have failed to appreciate that there *are* two.

The third principal member of Middle East command is Muhammad Kho'ansari, the top-level liaison officer between Ayatollah Khomeini and President Gaddafi. By virtue of his job as head of Syrian military intelligence, Colonel Ghazi Kenaan is also a member. Colonel Kenaan was the officer responsible for the massacre of 20,000 opponents of the Assad régime in Hama, Syria, in February 1982.

Connected with Middle East command and largely run by it is Islamic Jihad of Egypt, whose leader is Amar el-Masri, an Egyptian. It was Islamic Jihad of Egypt, an Egyptian-Libyan group, which assassinated President Sadat. Its principal mission now is to murder President Mubarak or in some other way bring down his régime.

All activity against Arab leaders accused of being unIslamic or 'unfaithful to Allah', or of being in league with the West, is organized by the Middle East command. Its structure is particularly well known to Arab heads of state because one member

of the Shi'a hierarchy in Iran withdrew from the
plan to wage jihad and warned Muslim leaders of
the plots against their lives. He is Ayatollah
Muhammad-Taqi Qumi, the only senior member
of the Iranian religious establishment to be himself
a target for assassination. He condones jihad against
the West and against Christians generally.

Apart from the Supreme Co-ordinating Council
there is a Jihad Commission though it is not clear
to what extent its functions overlap those of the
Council. The main members of the Commission
are:

Hashemi Rafsanjani, Speaker of the Iranian
parliament.
Ayatollah Khoeini, Khomeini's Leipzig-trained
personal representative to Mecca.
Moussavi Khamenei, President of the Islamic
Republic of Iran.
Ali Akhbar Velayati, Foreign Minister of Iran; he
studied at Johns Hopkins University, USA.
Seyyed Muhammad Khatemi, Iran's propaganda
minister.
An ayatollah who represents the Savama, Khomeini's intelligence service.
A Pasdaran (Revolutionary Guards) leader; he was
once a member of the Shah's intelligence service,
Savak.
Ayatollah Janati, chief of an organization known as
the Council of Fighting Clergy. This group is
believed to have great influence among the
ayatollahs.

Sayyed Muhammad Bagher Hakim, former head
of the Supreme Council of the Islamic Revolution
of Iraq.

'Mirshashem' – the nom de guerre of the chief of
the Jihad Commission. Mirshashem could well be
Hussein Moussavi, whom I interviewed in
Baalbek.

Abbas Zamani, probably the key KGB man on
the Commission. A good deal is known about
Zamani. Originally a teacher, he served time in
prison after 1972 and came under the direction of
Ayatollah Telagani. In that year he helped to
organize the Jihad organization in Lebanon and
was a founder of Hezbollah, 'Party of Allah', in
Lebanon. Returning to Iran he helped to over-
throw the last government formed under the Shah.
As head of the Pasdaran he threw out Bani Sadr
and Sadegh Ghotzadeh. Khomeini sent him to
Pakistan to 'mediate' with President Zia al-Huq.
He is believed to be responsible for Zia's 'Law of
Islamization' in Pakistan.

In each target country the Commission has an
agency whose work is dictated by local circumstances. In Britain part of the direction comes from the
Iranian mission but it is believed that jihad is also
directed through the Islamic Foundation, called in
Arabic Ahl-al-Beit ('Members of the House'). The
Foundation's activities are non-violent and are
aimed more at widespread propaganda for the
Islamic 'cause'. It produces a wide range of 'educa-
tional' materials.

In France the Iranian Embassy directs terror by

hiring professional terrorists and assassins. In the murder of the Iranian opposition leader General Oveissi both the 'Carlos' gang and Abu Nidal, the Palestinian terrorist, were involved.

Of the many groups linked with the Supreme Co-ordinating Council and Islamic Jihad and its Supreme Co-ordinating Council the most powerful and influential are Amal (the Lebanese Shi'a organization led by Nabih Berri); The Revolutionary Organization of Socialist Muslims (which is a front for the Palestinian terrorist Abu Nidal); the Islamic Liberation Organization and Islamic Unification, under Said Shaban; Islamic Liberation Organization, whose driving force is Hojatalislam Ahmad Fahri; Revolutionary Mujuhideen Organization of Iraq, led by Muhammad Ahmad al-Heidari; the Kuwait Islamic Liberation Movement, controlled by Abbas Mohri; and the Organization for the Liberation of the Arabian Peninsula, led by Ahmed Nekhvale, which is dedicated to the overthrow of all Arab monarchs.

Various affiliated groups have regional functions. For instance, the Islamic Call Party (al-Dawa al-Islamia) is responsible for bringing about, through jihad, the downfall of the Iraqi régime and some of the sheikhdoms in the Arabian Gulf. Its members are Shi'a people of Iraq who are opposed to Saddam Hussein. While most of its attacks are against Arab targets several of its members are among the 17 held in Kuwaiti prisons for the attacks in December 1983 against the US and French embassies in Kuwait.

Generally, Islamic Jihad is administered from a drab three-storey building in Teheran, opposite the former US embassy. It is called the Taleghani Centre and it is protected by Revolutionary Guards.

Thousands of young Shi'a militants have flocked to the centre. Many went there to take up religious studies but were then induced to attend 'liberation' camps for military training. A senior officer of the Taleghani Centre, Taki Moudarrissi, in September 1984 told the French magazine *Jeune Afrique*, 'In one week I can assemble 500 faithful ready to throw themselves into suicide operations.'

The basic training course for assassins selected by Moudarrissi and his assistant, Haideri, lasts three months and is carried out under the guidance of Palestinian, Libyan, North Korean, Pakistani and South Yemeni instructors, as well as specialists from the Revolutionary Guards.

Teheran has three training centres, with others at Ahwaz, Shiraz, Mashad, Qum and Busheir. The recruits learn basic military skills but have special training in explosives and in the mechanics of the vans and lorries used in bombing attacks.

In August 1985 a new Iranian unit, the 110th Independent Brigade or 'Partisans' Brigade', became operational for use in Europe. The title does not indicate any kind of formal military structure but is in keeping with the Iranian preference for combat-like labels.

The Supreme Co-ordinating Council had earlier chosen Vienna as the command post for Western

Europe and the Iranian ambassador to Austria,
Mehdi Ahari Mostafavi, became director for activities in Western Europe when he took up his duties
as ambassador in mid-1985.

Mostafavi was first trained in terror activities at
a camp run by George Habash's Popular Front for
the Liberation of Palestine (PFLP), a component
group of the PLO. Later he graduated from the
Patrice Lumumba University in Moscow, a university specializing in subversive studies. Before he
went to Austria he was Chief of Department Three
(Western Europe) for the Iranian Ministry of Foreign Affairs.

His principal targets are Iranian organizations
which want to overthrow the Khomeini régime.
These include groups which support restoration of
the monarchy under the 'Young Shah', as well as
Communist Party groups, Kurdish liberation cells
and the 'Shah's Army,' which is led by former
officers of the old régime.

Because the Tudeh (Communist) Party of Iran
has support groups in England, France, Italy and
the United States, the much strengthened Iranian
jihad network aims at targets in these countries.
During 1984–85 hatred of Britain grew among
revolutionary Islamic leaders. They accused Britain
of 'harbouring criminals' (the anti-Khomeini Iranians), of supporting the 'foul Saddam Hussein' of
Iraq and of 'friendship with the Great Satan,'
meaning the US.

Following the British government's announcement that it would be selling armaments and

aircraft to Saudi Arabia and Jordan the Khomeini régime upgraded Britain to 'Great Satan' class; both these Arab countries are regarded as 'unIslamic'.

Melli University near Evin, north-west of Teheran, and Shiraz University have training faculties at which revolutionaries and terrorists from all over the world are trained. The centres, which have the cover label 'Revolutionary Research Faculty,' were established in 1982 but their existence was not known in the West until late 1984.

Melli, with 1,000 'students' enrolled in the terrorist department, is the more important. Its intake in 1985–86 included terrorists from the IRA, the Syrian branch of the PLO and the secret Armenian army, ISALA. Others came from Sri Lanka, Senegal, Brazil, North Korea, Paraguay and Mexico.

The students at Shiraz University are mostly Shi'a Muslims; they include Iraqis, Lebanese, Saudis and Kuwaitis, as well as native Iranians. In 1986 some Russian Muslims were enrolled.

The university courses were organized by Ayatollah Sheikh Fazlollal Mehdi-Zadeh Mahellati, Ayatollah Azari Ghomi and Ayatollah Sheikh Hadi Ghaffari, leader of the Hezbollah anti-riot force. The Iraqi mullah Taki Moudarrissi, earlier mentioned as principal of the Taleghani Centre, is one of the most important course directors. He lectures on the use of psychology in jihad and has said that when the 'time is right' he will blow up the White House in Washington.

Experts give courses in subversion, disguise, blackmail and intimidation. Certain students are

taught how to use advanced techniques to gain
access to computer data banks. Guest lecturers –
including Europeans – speak about ways of exploiting politicians, priests and journalists in their
respective countries.

Melli University gives practical training in explosives and sabotage at extra-mural camps in Firuz-
koor and Mandari'yeh. Shiraz University uses a
similar camp at Persopolis.

In 1984–85 about 300 young foreign women, all
converted to Islam, were well trained in Iran for
terrorist and suicide missions. It has never been
envisaged that all such students will actually be
used on such a mission but when so many are
trained the best can be selected. In 1985 the
women included 30 from Northern Ireland, 6 from
Britain, 45 from Central America and an unspeci-
fied number from the US. One of the Irish girls
was said to be Bernadette Dolan, who later became
an employee of Teheran TV. Leader of the women
until 1986 was Mrs Zahra Rahnavard Moussavi,
aged 30, wife of the Iranian Prime Minister.

While President Gaddafi co-operates with the
Iranian and Syrian jihad organizations and heavily
funds them he has his own separate holy war
command structure. This is partly because Gaddafi
has always liked to operate independently but also
because many of his targets are Libyan 'traitors' –
men who oppose his régime from abroad. His
agents relentlessly hunt them down; they have
killed in Britain, France, West Germany, Holland,
Italy, the United States and in Arab countries.

Simultaneously Gaddafi has two other general holy war targets – the more moderate Arab leaders and what he habitually refers to as 'the infidel world beyond'. By this term he means the world at large which is not Islamic.

He has established 'cultural centres' very far from Libya, as Bangkok in Thailand and Melbourne in Australia. These centres are centres for holy war activity – such as subversion, propaganda, corruption of local officials, conversion to Islam. Despite his notorious record for interference in other nations' affairs Gaddafi has been remarkably successful in convincing some governments that his centres exist purely to explain Libyan culture.

Syrian jihadic leaders also have their own aims, apart from those they share with non-Arab Iran. Its régime has systematically embarked on narco-jihad – holy war with narcotic drugs. Ever since Syria gained control of Lebanon its leaders have been able to take over the manufacture and distribution of heroin and opium – as well as the traditional Arab hashish.

Under the supervision of General Rifaat Assad, younger brother of the president, the army has protected the drug convoys and the processing plants in northern Lebanon. Most of the final product finishes up in Western Europe and in the United States. During 1985 the Italian and Spanish police in particular were alarmed by the quantity of drugs reaching the streets and their investigations showed that personnel from Syrian embassies were heavily involved.

While a major purpose of the drug trade is to make money to buy more and more arms it is equally important to the Islamic Commission and the Supreme Co-ordinating Council as a way of destabilizing the West. It is known that Ayatollah Khomeini encouraged the export of narcotic drugs, as 'an agent of social destruction,' to the United States in particular.

The PLO has been trafficking in narcotics since the early 1970s but its prime purpose was to raise money. In 1983 Fatah, the main PLO group, split in two; half stayed loyal to Yasser Arafat while the other half, led by Abu Musa, came under Syrian control. Through its offices world-wide the PLO had a network of agents and helpers, many of whom were taken over by the Syrians. Since that time there has been evidence that the Syrians have used their part of the PLO to develop their drug outlets.[1]

[1] The Spanish magazine *Tiempo*, 11.11.85, analyses Syrian involvement in the drug traffic in an article entitled *Trafico de heroina: la policia investiga a la embajada siria*. The Italian journal *Famiglia Cristiana*, No. 45 1985, covered the same topic in *Arriva dal Libano; La Droga di Stato*.

CHAPTER EIGHT

'Great Satan' – and smaller devils

'The battle that is being fought today in the Muslim World is between Western materialism and Islam, the last of the messages from Allah. On one side there is agnosticism and on the other the Divine Law . . . this is the last great struggle between religion and irreligiousness after which the world will swing full-scale towards one side or the other.'

This statement was made by Abul Hasan Ali Nadwi, a Pakistani, writing[1] just before Ayatollah Khomeini returned to Iran from exile in 1979.

'For a full century,' wrote Nadwi, 'the West has been preying on the hearts and minds of Muslims. It has played havoc with its scepticism, doubt and disbelief. The transcendental truths have been trampled underfoot by the materialistic concepts of political science and economics . . .'

Because of the evil influences of the West on the world of Islam, Nadwi concluded, Islam was fighting 'the holiest of holy wars.' This expresses the view of virtually all the Islamic scholars and theologians who formulate the policy and strategy of holy war.

For them no nation more exemplifies the

[1] In his pamphlet *The New Menace and its Answer*, Academy of Islamic Research and Publications, Lucknow, India, 1977.

'materialistic concepts of political science and economics' than the United States. These two fundamental aspects of Western life are inimical to Islam because they pose many theories and propose many experiments and solutions. In contrast, traditional Islam accepts only the politics and economics of the *Koran* as set down by Muhammad. For instance, the Shah of Iran was considered evil because he placed himself above the theologians, beyond their advice and in the hands of the West.

As Khomeini was growing in power he labelled the United States the 'Great Satan,' an epithet he frequently repeated to justify his actions against the Americans. No punishment could be too severe for the Great Satan, hence the seizing of the American embassy in Teheran and the holding of hostages, the later murders of Americans in various places, the killing of Iranians alleged to have collaborated with the Great Satan and threats to murder American leaders.

Khomeini and the Iranian ayatollahs, as well as Gaddafi and his supporters, and other Islamic zealots from Saudi Arabia, Pakistan and Morocco accuse the West, and particularly the Americans, of corrupting Muslims.

Under the Shah Iran had become the most powerful nation in the Middle East and was popularly known as the 'policeman of the Persian Gulf.' Khomeini wanted Iran to remain powerful but he resented the nation's dependence on the United States for its military might. He resented even more the close collaboration between Iran's gener-

als and American generals. He declared that the
Shah had 'sold himself' to the Americans and was
therefore guilty of crimes against Allah; he meant
that a Muslim as powerful as the Shah was committing apostasy in associating himself closely with
Christians.

Khomeini was especially angry over the influence of American culture on Iranian women, in
teaching them that the sexes are equal and in
encouraging them to wear 'indecent' Western dress
and make-up, and to mix with men. The Shah had
permitted all this and much more, so the ayatollahs
hated him. Khomeinism blames the United States
for giving Muslims a taste for popular music,
Western poetry, dancing, drinking, gambling and
other things forbidden or said to be forbidden by
the *Koran*.

In their zeal to combat this corruption the ayatollahs have closed departments in colleges,
banned certain subjects, dismissed teachers and
have insisted on segregated classes for female students who had previously attended joint classes.
Following the Iranian lead, in many Muslim countries mobs led by bearded fundamentalist activists
have burned down newspaper offices after the
publication of articles deemed offensive to Islam,
while many books and films have fallen foul of self-
appointed Islamic censors. This willingness to use
violence together with righteous fury over 'insults
to religion' has been effective in mobilizing urban
mobs in Muslim countries to intimidate those who
hold different views. Even the centuries-old

custom of raising pigs for their own use by Christian Arabs has been the object of demonstrations and harassment by fundamentalists; they abhor this meat, which is forbidden to Muslims.

Unable to attack the Great Satan on his home ground, Islamic Jihad and its various groups have concentrated on attacking Americans abroad. In 1983 American citizens and property were the targets of 41 per cent of terrorist attacks worldwide; of 500 attacks 205 were against the US. In 1983 271 Americans were killed and 116 were wounded compared to 7 killed in 1982. During 1984 17 Americans were killed and 40 wounded in holy war attacks. For 1985 the figures were 19 and 42 respectively. The majority of victims were diplomats and their families and servicemen. All were attacked outside the United States.

These statistics do not take into account the many hostages held by Islamic Jihad. Holding hostages continuously is a basic part of jihad strategy because they provide a base for political bargaining. William Buckley, an official of the US embassy in Beirut, was kidnapped on 16 March 1984 and until his death late in 1985 he was the longest-held American captive.

The hostages are frequently the basis for demands and threats. For instance, in May 1985 photographs of four Americans and two Frenchmen, both diplomats, were published in several Beirut daily newspapers, together with an ominous warning. Unless the government of Kuwait agreed to release 17 Islamic Jihad terrorists in prison there for bombing the US and French embassies in December 1983 the American captives would suffer 'catastrophic consequences' and their captors would terrorize America and France 'forever.' The same group had hijacked a Kuwaiti airliner in December 1984 and killed two Americans on board in a futile effort to win freedom for their terrorist friends.

American priests and academics working abroad are also targets for Islamic jihad. In January 1984 Malcolm Kerr, aged 52, president of the American University of Beirut (AUB) was shot dead by two gunmen for no reason other than that he was an American. In a broadcast, Islamic Amal, the group responsible, announced that as Dr Kerr was 'a child of the Great Satan and leader of an American institution which has no business in Lebanon' he had been selected for death to show the American administration that it 'cannot win the war'.

The AUB was founded in 1865 and there is hardly an Arab government which does not contain at least one graduate. Kerr had devoted his life to Arab culture and education and had ceaselessly worked to promote trust and friendship between the West and the Arab world. His murder shocked his many Arab friends. His predecessor as president of the AUB, David Dodge, had been kidnapped in July 1982 and held for a year before being released.

Early in 1980 American FBI agents and other law enforcement officers discovered that at least $5 million had been smuggled into the US to support

Iranian revolutionary protest and propaganda efforts. Funds had been sent from Iran in diplomatic pouches with international couriers and through foreign banks; some money had been raised in the US through the sale of hashish and heroin. The money was to recruit, transport, feed and train Iranian students and black Muslims. At the heart of the movement the FBI found a cadre of about 50 people dedicated to the principles of the Iranian revolution. One of them was Daoud Salahuddin, who was accused of murdering the leader of an anti-Khomeini Iranian faction in Bethesda, Maryland. Salahuddin's group is known as the Islamic Guerrillas in America and according to a leaflet which it produced the group advocates the destruction of its enemies 'by any means, whether lawful or not.'

Since 1980 large amounts of money have reached the US to finance operations against the many anti-Khomeini Iranians who have fled from Iran.

If the United States is the Great Satan in the eyes of Islamic Jihad the countries of Europe are lesser devils only because they are under the influence of the Americans. Khomeini was sweeping, as always, in his denunciation of the Europeans in 1979.

'Europe is nothing but a collection of unjust dictatorships,' he declared. 'All of humanity must strike these troublemakers with an iron fist if it wishes to regain its tranquillity. If Islamic civilization had governed the West we would no longer have to put up with these barbaric goings-on

unworthy even of wild animals . . . The leaders of
our country have been so influenced by the West
that they have regulated the standard time of our
country upon that of Europe. [Greenwich Mean
Time.] What a nightmare!'

In 1980 Islamic Jihad singled out for attack
France, Britain and Italy, in that order, as priority
targets for jihad. Italy was declared to be a special
kind of Satan because the Pope lives in Rome. The
Iranian ayatollahs as a whole accept Khomeini's
assessment of the Pope as 'the leader of a false
religion.' Gaddafi has said that, 'This man [the
Pope] does not recognize Muhammad as the final
messenger of Allah; he is therefore an enemy of
Islam.'

Later Italy (with Austria) was placed much lower
on Islamic Jihad's hit list – though they remained
high on the Libyan list. The holy war leaders found
the leaders of Italy and Austria were 'co-operative'
and they were able to establish Islamic Jihad bases
in these countries. The Austrian and Italian toler-
ance of holy war terrorists in their countries was
ill-founded. Holy war terrorism struck in both
States, when gunmen attacked passengers at the
national airports on 27 December 1985.

France is considered only marginally less guilty
of crimes against Allah than the US. More specifically, the French have committed crimes against
'Allah's messenger' – Ayatollah Khomeini – by
supporting Iraq in the Iran–Iraq Gulf War. In
addition, the French had once possessed an empire
in Islamic lands – Algeria, Tunisia, Morocco, and

Syria and Lebanon. Because of this history of colonialism any French political act within the Islamic world is seen as suspicious by Islamic Jihad, which has found many targets in France, such as trains and railway stations, embassies and great stores, synagogues and restaurants.

In northern France in mid-1984 French police arrested three holy war terrorists who had been expelled from London a month earlier. They were a Moroccan named Chraibi and Algerians Yahya Gouasmi and Redgradj. On 30 June they were set free without explanation, although they were important men in an Iranian-led network directed by Abofazal Beheshti, nephew of an ayatollah killed in factional fighting in Iran. Beheshti was involved in smuggling arms between Belgium and France. The sudden release of the terrorists coincided with the visit to Paris of Sadegh Tabatahai, Khomeini's special envoy and an arms dealer. He was seeking to 'normalize' relations between France and Iran; that is, he was trying to induce the French not to sell arms and aircraft to Iraq. The French for their part hoped to induce Iran to stop its holy war terrorism against France. Neither side had any success.

Britain is also considered a 'Satan'. The main crime of the British is their political support for the Americans and their 'interference' in the Arabian Gulf. For instance, the army of Oman is largely trained, led and armed by Britain. Islamic Jihad regards this as a form of colonialism. A British naval presence in the Gulf – to protect British shipping

from attack by the Gulf War belligerents – is also
seen as a warlike act against Islam. Because of the
high standard of British security Islamic Jihad has
found it difficult to hit targets in the United Kingdom; as a substitute it has sent assassins to kill
British officials abroad. In March 1984 they murdered Mr Ken Whitty, a deputy director of the
British Council in Athens. In December 1984 Mr
Percy Norris, British deputy high commissioner in
Bombay, was killed by two men as he was being
driven to work. The Revolutionary Organization of
Socialist Muslims claimed responsibility for both
killings. This organization is linked both to the Abu
Nidal Palestinian terrorist group and to Islamic
Jihad. It has exploded bombs at British Council
offices in Beirut and Baghdad. In holding British
people as hostages, Terry Waite and John
McCarthy particularly, Islamic Jihad hopes to use
them in exchange for Muslim terrorists in British
gaols, principally those guilty of the attempted
murder of the Israeli ambassador in London,
Shlomo Argov.

Britain happens to be Iran's second most important trading partner in the Middle East after Saudi
Arabia; during 1987 goods worth nearly £800 million were sold to Iran. However, this important
economic link gives Britain no protection against
the excesses of holy war.

President Gaddafi, no less than the Iranian ayatollahs, regards the Western countries as Satans,
though except to echo Khomeini he has not himself
used that epithet. For Gaddafi the Western nations
are imperialists, colonialists and part of a 'Zionist

conspiracy.' Gaddafi's role in jihad is described in Chapter 12 but it should be said here that his principal targets are those Libyans living abroad who are alleged to be conspiring against his regime. Several have been killed in Britain, France, Italy, Spain, West Germany and Austria. His next priority is to fight the West by giving military and financial aid to subversive groups within the Western states, such as the IRA in Northern Ireland and the Black Panthers, among others, in the US, and Action Directe in France. Thirdly, he wages jihad against Israel by training, financing, equipping various terrorist groups, mainly those allied with the PLO. Should they survive an exploit, such as a hijacking, he gives them refuge.

Colonel Gaddafi came to power in 1969 by overthrowing King Idris. In 1972 when I interviewed him at some length in Tripoli he was still in a state of executive euphoria and white hot with ambition to reform the Arabic and Islamic worlds, to spread the word of Islam and to make his large state with its tiny population militarily powerful. With money pouring in from the sale of Libyan oil he had the means to attempt to realize some of his ambitions.

At the end of our interview he presented me with a poster, in an ornate silver frame, showing him in the act of embracing the entire Arab world; it is illustrated in this book. Later he was advised that the poster, which had not been widely circulated, could be compromising: Other Arab rulers might not rejoice in his desire to take over their countries. A Libyan official approached me and asked if I would return my copy but I declined. It was, after all, an historic document depicting jihad.

While it was very difficult to gain access to Gaddafi in 1972 it was easy enough once in his presence to induce him to talk. Looking at the poster I said, 'This seems to show that you want to rule an Arab empire.' The word 'empire' displeased him and he corrected me. 'I will guide the Islamic world.'

'Suppose the other Islamic countries do not want you to guide them?'

'I will persuade my brothers that I have greater vision than they do,' Gaddafi said. 'One way or another I will persuade them.'

'Through jihad if necessary?'

He was impatient with this question and explained at length that for him jihad had been incessant since the 'glorious day of liberation' in September 1969; it was not something which he declared at some particular time. Jihad would go on until Islam was 'triumphant.'

Through television and radio the Iranians and Libyans wage a constant campaign of hatred and ridicule against the West. These programmes are later seen and heard in most Islamic countries. The plan is to show the United States as corrupt, Britain as decadent and the French as stupid. Muslim, generally Arab, camera crews frequently tour the West to film aspects of Western life which can be presented as evidence of corruption, decadence and stupidity, for instance, race riots, punk gatherings, drug addicts, and urban crime. Upper class social events are examples of degeneracy and decadence, scenes at the Wall Street stock exchange illustrate corruption and a French rugby match is filmed and edited in such a way that it appears ludicrous. In all cases the commentary is hostile. Throughout all programmes there is the underlying theme of 'Western irreligious materialism', with attacks on the evils identified by Abul Nadwi and exploited by the Iranian ayatollahs – 'political science and economics.'

CHAPTER NINE

And Great Sinners

While one holy war campaign is being waged against Great Satans another campaign is in progress against Great Sinners. The Satans are foreign unbelievers while the Sinners are those Muslims within Islam declared to be guilty of various un-Islamic or anti-Islamic practices. The greatest of them are the monarchs who sin just by being monarchs, according to the fundamentalists who lead the jihad. The least of them are those ordinary men who do not fully practise their faith.

Fundamentalism is really a euphemistic term for fanaticism or radical puritanism but fundamentalists themselves only rarely accept the term fundamentalist. They prefer to call themselves Islamists. By this they mean that they are merely doing what is correct and proper for Muslims to do.

An Afghani resistance leader, B. Rabbani, says, 'Fundamentalist is a word we do not use. We who follow the right path are Islamists, that is to say, for us Islam is a driving force which concerns every aspect of our life . . . we are, above all else, believers.'

For fundamentalists, while all Muslims are members of the world of Islam, they are not necessarily Islamists. According to fundamentalists many Muslims are not true believers. Those at fault include all men guilty of breaches of their Islamic faith; all those who have relations of any kind with non-Muslims – unless such a relationship is undertaken for the benefit of Islam; all men who set themselves up as princes and kings and those who serve monarchs; all men guilty of any activity proscribed by Islam, such as drinking alcohol, attending night clubs and gambling.

Much of the influence of the leading fundamentalists, such as the Iranian ayatollahs, the Shi'a revolutionaries and Pakistani and Egyptian Islamic scholars stems from their being able to articulate popular grievances on political, social and economic issues within the Muslim world. This influence has grown into great political power. The result is that during the 1970s and 1980s those secular-minded and modernist governments within the world of Islam have been forced on to the defensive by the rising tide of Islamic fundamentalism.

Muslim fundamentalists rarely hold power in government – with the notable exception of Iran – but their demands, when presented as 'Islamic', have been accepted by governments which are anxious to appease the protesters. As a result horse-racing, betting, sale and consumption of alcohol and the establishment of city night clubs have been banned or restricted in some states.

In numerous petty ways daily life in Muslim cities has been affected by the insistent and threatening demands of activitists who want reforms. Changes in dress are probably the most dramatic and surprising development as far as women are concerned.

The tremendous growth of cities, with millions of villagers uprooted, as in Egypt, Iran, Pakistan and elsewhere, is a major factor in fundamentalism. The hectic pace of change is unsettling and has led to political demands by new urban groups. The organized power of the new city dwellers in Teheran and other large Iranian cities played a major part in the Iranian revolution, overthrowing a ruler 'grossly entrenched in power' – as well as being backed by the United States. This new class in Iran continues to be a force in the Islamic revolution. The rapid urban growth in many Muslim countries has created a huge underclass of aspiring townsmen, often living in slum conditions. They resent the privileged Westernized élite whose lifestyle of material comfort, secular tastes and Western dress is a permanent affront to the religious puritans.

The popular identification of Islam itself with the poor and the exploited classes of Muslims has greatly helped the leaders of the holy war movement; it has made it easier for them to rouse the Muslim masses into political fervour.

The zealots who guide holy war within the Muslim world want, above all, to 'purify' Islam; this is the term they repeatedly use. Purification demands the removal of the leading sinners, by murder if necessary. Purification also requires that Islamic states should become theocracies and therefore controlled, if not actually governed, by the imams, ayatollahs and mullahs.

One of the most serious warnings of punishments being prepared for the 'Great Sinners' came from the only member of the Shi'a hierarchy to leave Iran for exile. He is Ayatollah Muhammad-Taqi Qumi, who was appalled by what he called 'the Muslim thirst for Muslim blood.' Seeking refuge in Egypt, he sent a message to Muslim leaders throughout the world, warning them of 'sinister plots' and calling for urgent action to stop the 'incipient bloodshed.'

The principal target of holy war within Islam is Saudi Arabia. The reasons are obvious. Saudi Arabia is not a theocracy and the *ulema* (priests) while powerful as a class are merely junior partners to the Saudi king and the leading princes. Apart from this affront to the fundamentalists, the 5,000-strong royal family has a tight monopoly of power and state riches. In addition, some of the princes are blatantly corrupt and immoral.

To the world of Islam, Saudi Arabia is uniquely important because the holiest places of Islam are within its borders. Therefore, the fundamentalists say, Saudis generally must set an example in Islamic purity. The length to which the holy war leaders are prepared to go in their campaign of purification was shown on 20 November 1979 – the first day of the new century in the Muslim calendar, year 1400. An armed band of insurgents seized the Great Mosque of Mecca, the holiest place of Islam, to which Muslims the world over turn five times a day in prayer. The taking of the mosque was an act of sacrilege without parallel.

The Mecca insurgents were led by a young fanatic, Juhaiman al-Oteibi, who had been educated at Medina University, Saudi Arabia, an ultra-conservative theological seminary. Al-Oteiba's group believed that one of their companions, Muhammad al-Quraishi, was the long-awaited Mahdi, who would deliver the Muslims throughout Islam from their wicked, immoral and corrupt rulers. They regarded even the Saudi *ulema* as sinners, accusing them of having sold out to the monarchy.

Al-Oteiba and others of his group had been manipulated by both Khomeini agents and Gaddafi agents, each anxious to bring about a revolution in Saudi Arabia. Khomeini wanted to gain control of the holy places by using the 500,000 Shi'as living in eastern Saudi Arabia as his shock troops. Gaddafi, himself ambitious to lead a political Islam, wanted the status which control of Mecca would give him. Both arch conspirators damned the Saudi establishment for its 'sins against Allah'. Neither accepted the claim by the Al-Oteiba group that the Mahdi would come from its ranks; all that mattered to Khomeini and Gaddafi was that these mostly young men were available for the Mecca attack.

After a bloody siege the insurgents were captured and executed but the shock of the event greatly damaged the prestige of the Saudi monarchy. It was followed by Shi'a riots within the country, but news of them was suppressed. The Shi'a ferocity was fanned by a new radio station, calling itself 'The Voice of the Islamic Revolution

in Saudi', which began broadcasting from Iran. The
voice of Ayatollah Khomeini urged workers in the
oilfields to revolt in holy war against the 'Saudi
sinners and oppressors who bring shame to the
holy places.' Many of the Shi'a community used
modern weapons in this uprising, all of them
smuggled in from Iran and Kuwait. One ayatollah,
broadcasting from Iran, urged his fellow Shi'as 'to
kill a prince and find Paradise.' The Saudi army
broke the uprising but the royal family was left
shaken and afraid.

Shock led the ruling princes to re-assess Saudi
policies. A new more assertive foreign policy developed. The princes wanted to show the fundamentalist zealots that they were not the 'hirelings' of
the United States. Declaring themselves to be pure
and pious Muslims, they asked their own *ulema* to
tell the jihadic leaders that they were not 'sinners'.
That they considered this step necessary was an
indication of their anxiety over holy war.

Every year since 1979 the threat of holy war has
been obvious during the pilgrimage season (*hajj*) to
Mecca and Medina. With millions of Muslim pilgrims congregating for the holy rites the jihad high
command uses the occasion to demonstrate their
power. Huge contingents of Iranian pilgrims
engage in noisy and provocative demonstrations.
Carrying political/religious posters, they distribute
leaflets which criticize the Saudi rulers and praise
Khomeini and other leading ayatollahs. The Iranians, together with Syrians and Libyans, arrange
protest meetings among the crowds – an unprece-

dented activity during the holy season – at which they preach against the 'un-Islamic' Saudi regime. All the other Muslim kings and princes are also attacked. In 1984 the Iranians numbered 150,000 and in 1985, despite efforts by the Saudis to restrict the Shi'a contingent, they numbered closer to 200,000. During the 1986 *hajj* the Saudis arrested 100 Iranians who were smuggling explosives into Mecca. In July 1987, during the *hajj*, Iranian holy war fanatics started riots in which more than 400 people were killed in Mecca. Moderate Islam was shocked.

The Saudi rulers have tried to resolve their dilemma by becoming fundamentalist themselves and declaring their own version of holy war. Saudi Arabia set out to dominate the Organization of the Islamic Conference (OIC), which had been founded in 1969. Because it is based in Jeddah, Saudi Arabia, it was not difficult for the princes to take over OIC, which has 13 subsidiary organizations, seven affiliated institutions and six specialized committees. It has tried to provide a framework for positive action in ending disputes and wars between Muslim states – with conspicuous failure.

The OIC, under Saudi patronage, has been more successful in promoting Islamic banking and economic co-operation between rich and poor Muslim states. At the third Islamic Summit Conference in 1981, held at Taif in Saudi Arabia, the Saudis offered one billion dollars towards a three-billion dollar programme. A proliferation of Islamic conferences funded by Saudi organizations takes place each year in various cities of Muslim countries. The aim is to show to the Islamic world that Saudi Arabia is a leader in fundamentalist activity.

The Saudis have persuaded other Muslim states to move towards what the Saudis claim are authentic Islamic policies, by adopting the laws of the Shari'a and abandoning Western models and codes. Pakistan, Sudan and Mauretania, for instance, reverted to the Shari'a with its harsh punishments, such as stoning to death for adulterous women and hand-lopping for thieves. The Saudis commonly use these punishments, as do the Iranians and Libyans.

Many near-bankrupt military regimes in Muslim countries have gone some way in applying Shari'a laws and have promised gradual Islamization of their societies – and in return they have received large loans and grants from Saudi-based institutions. The Saudis have rewarded, for instance, any country which abandons the Sunday weekly holiday imposed by Christian colonial administrations and substitutes the Muslim Friday sabbath.

Saudi funds from state and private sources promote a wide range of contacts at different levels, from the teaching of Arabic in non-Arab countries to the building of mosques and cultural centres as well as provision for scholarships for foreign students to study Islamic subjects in Saudi Arabia itself. The Muslim World League is active in these fields.

Propaganda is carried on from Riyadh on a scale comparable to Moscow's effort to spread commu-

nism. Islamic radio programmes are funded in
many languages. At the end of 1984 a printing
press was opened in Medina, with the capacity to
produce seven million copies of the *Koran* each
year. As well as copies of the *Koran* in fine Arabic
calligraphy the press prints translations for the
many millions of Muslims who cannot read Arabic.
The centre produces 300,000 sets of audio and
video cassettes annually, at a total cost of $140
million.

Despite all the evidence which the Saudis can
produce to show that they are widely and deeply
involved in their own conservative type of jihad
they are not out of danger from the more rigorous
and aggressive Shi'as, whether they are Iranian,
Lebanese, Bahreini, Iraqi, North Yemeni or Pakistani. Ayatollah Montazeri, Khomeini's successor
as spiritual leader of Islamic holy war, calls the
Saudi efforts 'acceptable but cosmetic.' Whatever
the Saudi rulers do in the cause of jihad, the fact
remains that they are part of a monarchy, which
puts the temporal king above the spiritual ayatollah. Fundamentalists (Islamists) insist that the
house of Saud must be destroyed whatever 'bribes'
it offers.

This applies to all the other monarchs of whatever ranks, from sultan to king. All have adopted
the Saudi stratagem of trying to avoid becoming
targets and victims of holy war by waging holy war.
It is unlikely to save them because the men of the
Islamic Jihad high command are unforgiving.

Many more acts of holy war against Saudi Arabia

and the other monarchies take place than are reported. In fact, the great majority of 'incidents' are kept out of the newspapers. They include bombs left in the street, parcel bombs, sniping at policemen and soldiers, arson attacks on government buildings and property known to be owned by a member of the Saudi royal family, damage to mosques frequented by members of the royal family.

The Saudi rulers as well as King Hussein of Jordan and King Hassan of Morocco have sent religious and political emissaries to Teheran to explain that they do not oppose Islamic Jihad and that they too are committed to the 'great striving.' All such emissaries have been received with hostility and threats. King Fahd and King Hussein are on particularly weak ground because militarily and financially they support Iraq in its war against Iran. This means, in the eyes of the Iranian ayatollahs, that they are preventing the Iranian holy war against Iraq from reaching its 'just conclusion.'

The fundamentalists' greatest sinner of all within the Muslim world was President Sadat and he paid for his sins with his life – principally for making peace with the Jewish (Israeli) unbelievers. President Mubarak, Sadat's successor, was also declared a great sinner for not abrogating the peace treaty with Israel and for not introducing the Shari'a law to modern Egypt. Egypt generally was said by the fundamentalists to have sinned by giving sanctuary to the Shah of Iran when he fled from Iran. When he died of cancer in Egypt the fundamentalist leaders declared a 'day of rejoicing.'

Mubarak has opposed jihad in his country but has been unable to prevent the fundamentalists from gaining ground and exerting their influence. This is largely because the academics and theologians at Al Azhar University in Cairo have immense prestige – and many of them are fundamentalists. Some would not be distressed if Mubarak, like Sadat, fell to assassins' bullets.

An incident in the Sinai desert in October 1985 showed that the jihad message was coming across in Egypt. Seven Israeli tourists including three children approached an Egyptian border post to chat with the sergeant on duty there. Almost immediately he opened fire, hitting all the Israelis. At least four of the Israelis were only lightly wounded but needed medical help to stem their bleeding. The sergeant, Suleiman Khater, and the other Egyptians present refused to allow anybody to approach his victims to give medical help and the wounded bled to death.

The Egyptian authorities reported that Sergeant Khater had 'gone berserk' but on inquiry it was found that he was perfectly sane. He had shot the Israelis as 'unbelievers' on the authority of the *Koran* which urges Muslims to 'slay the infidels wherever you find them.' In any case, he had come under the influence of agents, believed to be Syrian, preaching jihad.

In December the Egyptian authorities tried Sergeant Khater for murder; found guilty, he was

sentenced to life imprisonment with hard labour.
Protest demonstrations began at once, particularly
among university students. Khater, they said, was
doing no more than his holy duty. Saudi newspapers applauded Khater's heroic act. He committed suicide in his cell.

Egyptian intellectuals are directly under attack
as part of jihad. The noted writer Yusuf Idris is
accused of atheism because of his belief in science.
He acknowledges that the influence of Islamic
fundamentalism on Egyptian culture has been 'tremendous' and predicts that eventually all intellectuals will have to leave Egypt because the
fundamentalists oppose fiction, cinema, theatre,
music and dance and cultural activities generally;
they are 'un-Islamic.'

A modernist Muslim scholar, Fazlur Rahman,
complains bitterly that fundamentalists appear to
have 'a divine mission to shut down Islamic intellectual life.' He would certainly have evidence to
support his claim. In many Muslim countries mobs
led by fundamentalists burn down newspaper
offices after the publication of articles deemed
offensive to Islam, while many books and films
have fallen foul of self-appointed Islamic censors.
While many members of the mob might be illiterate or semi-literate the rabble-rousers are generally
educated, but only in Islamic literature. They do
not recognize great world literature, only pure
Islamic writing, particularly religious books.

Within Islam are some genuinely modernist
Muslims who criticize fundamentalism and jihad.

For them the Islamic activists are fanatics and they label them *Ikhwan al-Shaitan* ('Brothers of Satan'). Some go so far as to call them fascists. There are superficially close parallels between the phenomenon of fascism and Muslim fundamentalism, such as the mystic cult of the charismatic leader; the class appeal to the lower middle classes; the exploitation of discontent, frustrations and economic insecurity; the foundation themes of authority, discipline, tradition and order; the intolerance of opposition; the readiness to use violence; the relegation of women to a strictly controlled role.

Fascism was not only fashionable but exciting and desirable in Egypt, Lebanon and India (before partition) when Muslim fundamentalism was spreading its roots through small groups. The Grand Mufti of Jerusalem was a fervent admirer of Adolf Hitler and became friendly with him.

But Muslim fundamentalism is different from fascism in some key respects. Fundamentalism is internationalist or pan-nationalist while fascism is ultra-nationalist. Fascism rejects religious authority while fundamentalism glories in it to a fanatical degree. Both fascism and fundamentalism are racist in their attitude towards their declared enemies; the enemies are 'inferior' people to both. However, Islamic fundamentalists base their claim to superiority on something special given to them by Allah or God in the *Koran*, thus making them unique in God's eyes. Fascists generally base their superiority on racial breeding and ancestry.

The most important characteristics shared by
fundamentalism and fascism is that both refuse to
negotiate or compromise and that both are without
pity. Enemies must submit totally or be crushed.

CHAPTER TEN

Car bombs, donkey bombs, body bombs . . . bombs

A British military policeman – a 'Red Cap' in the British Army – was outside the American embassy annex in East Beirut one day in September 1984, waiting for the British ambassador, David Miers, to finish a routine meeting with his American counterpart Reginald Bartholomew. It was the soldier's job to escort the ambassador back to his office.

Ever alert, the Red Cap glanced down the road and saw that a light-coloured Chevrolet van carrying Dutch diplomatic number plates had stopped by the guardroom. The van driver seemed to be having an argument with the gate guard. The driver fired a shot at the guard and accelerated towards the embassy.

The Red Cap realized at once that this was an attack of the kind which had killed American marines and French paras in Beirut the previous November. When the van was almost parallel with him the soldier fired five aimed shots at the driver through the door of the van. He saw the driver fall over and as he collapsed he pulled the steering wheel to the right.

Sliding out of control, the van hit an American truck parked in the driveway and exploded. The van and its driver were obliterated and the six-storey annex was destroyed; at least nine people were killed, all but two of them Lebanese, and nearly 40 were wounded. The explosion was so great that the military policeman was thrown 30 feet through the air, but without injury. If he had not fired the shots the van would have hit the front door of the embassy and the death toll would have been much greater.

An hour later the Beirut officer of the Agence France Press, the French news agency, and Reuters, the international agency, took calls from a man who spoke in cultured, classical Arabic. 'In the name of Allah, the compassionate, the merciful,' he said, 'the Islamic Jihad organization announces that it is responsible for blowing up a car fitted with explosives which was driven into the American embassy . . . We are the strongest and will remain the strongest.'

According to the employee who received the call at Agence France Press, the voice was the same as that which claimed responsibility for blowing up the American embassy in April 1983, when 63 people were killed. The news agencies get many such telephone messages; the caller nearly always speaks calmly and correctly and invariably begins his statement with the traditional 'In the name of Allah, the compassionate, the merciful . . .'

A week later an Islamic Jihad spokesman again telephoned the Western news agencies to give a message to President Reagan and to identify other targets. The message was: 'You, governor of the White House, await a painful blow . . . more painful than our blows against your embassy and your military headquarters in Beirut.' Islamic Jihad, he warned, was prepared to strike at major American cities and at US facilities in Latin America and Europe.

It was already known that Islamic Jihad's threats were not idle ones. On 12 December 1983 truck-bombs had hit American and French targets in Kuwait, killing five people and injuring 60 others. And the massacre of the American marines and French paras in Beirut was still fresh in the mind.

Early in 1984 Islamic Jihad established a new subsidiary organization, Arab-Islamic International, and appointed Ayatollah Montazeri, who is to be Khomeini's successor, and Ahmed Ben Bella, known as the 'Algerian Khomeini' to co-ordinate its activities. The function of Arab-Islamic International is to spread holy war in Europe and beyond and priority targets are American embassies, military headquarters and personnel. The field commanders of the new group first needed to establish stocks of explosive in Europe. Some of the couriers carrying explosives were caught during 1984. For instance, on 24 November Swiss police stopped a Lebanese Shi'a, Hani Hussein, at Zürich airport and found in his luggage two kilos of plastic explosive. From this lead other explosives were found in a locker at Zürich railway station. The packages were the last in a series of deliveries to build a car- or truck-bomb for a suicide action against the American Embassy in Rome.

Rome police arrested seven Lebanese Shi'as, all in their twenties, in Rome apartments. Propaganda literature for Islamic Jihad was found in the rooms. The arrests in Zürich and Rome might have prevented a suicide attack but it is likely that the seven 'students' were not the attack group but a logistical support network for this group.

Following their comparative failure in blowing up the American embassy in Beirut, Hezbollah (Party of Allah) threatened to hit British 'interests', people and property. This was partly in frustration at being baulked by the British military policeman, partly in line with jihad forward planning. At Hezbollah HQ in the Hay Mahdi suburb of West Beirut paintings and posters featured British symbols for the first time. One 10-foot painting showed an enormous Dracula-like figure with blood dripping from its fangs; the Union flag was draped over the left side of the head while the eyes were miniature US flags. Another poster showed the American, British, French and Soviet flags going up in flames; yet another illustrated a column of Shi'a holy war warriors marching 'towards Jerusalem.'

An official whose nom de guerre was Abdullah told Western reporters, 'We will burn the West out of the Islamic world. We have the words – *Allah akhbar* [Allah is great] and these words are more powerful than their big bombs. We can use our bodies and our blood. In the beginning nobody had heard of us. Now the big countries are afraid of Hezbollah and our martyrs.'

Islamic Jihad bombs have hit the French harder than most other people. The terrorists who killed five people and injured 39 with a bomb in a left-luggage locker at Marseilles railway station and another in a railway carriage of a high-speed train on New Year's Eve 1984 chose their timing carefully. The explosions occurred just as President Mitterand was stressing France's peace-keeping role in Lebanon in his traditional end-of-year broadcast to the nation. Two days later the 'Organization of the Arab Armed Struggle' claimed responsibility for the bombs. The New Year attacks followed a series of bombings in Paris, including one which wrecked a luxury restaurant.

These explosions too were apparently the work of the same gang, an offshoot of Islamic Jihad; its leaders are believed by French security chiefs to have links with the international terrorist known as Carlos (Ilich Ramirez Sanchez).

In February 1985 the capture of a would-be 16-year-old martyr, Muhammad Mahmoud Burro, a few hours before he was supposed to go on a suicide bombing mission, provided, for the first time, an opportunity to get into the mind of youths who consent to become such attackers and to learn something of the methods used to recruit them. Under questioning by his Israeli captors and in a separate interview with *The New York Times* Burro gave an account of his life, of his enlistment for the suicide mission and of the people he was working for.

The most striking aspect of Burro's account is

that although he is a Shi'a Muslim he comes from a
secular family background. He was not a fanatic
who wanted to kill himself in the cause of Islam or
anti-Zionism but was recruited for the suicide
mission through another means – blackmail.

He did not know beforehand most of the people
who recruited him or brought him to the point
where the car laden with explosives would be
delivered to him. His account indicated that planning and preparation for suicide attacks are carried
out by intelligence experts unknown to the driver,
who has been carefully recruited. In Burro's case,
the recruiters were from Lebanese Amal, whose
leader is Nabih Berri.

Burro told *The New York Times* journalist that a
few months earlier he was riding his motorcycle
and had an accident; he ran into the rear end of a
car. The incident, he said, eventually led him into
his suicide mission. In lawless Beirut, accidents are
often adjudicated on the spot between the two
drivers. Frequently the matter is resolved on the
basis of who draws a gun first. In this case, Burro
was clearly at fault. Seeking help, he contacted a
man named Abu Hassan, who was the Amal security chief in Beirut's southern suburbs.

'Abu Hassan closed the file on the accident,'
Burro said. It is not clear what Abu Hassan did,
but he got Burro out of trouble and put him in his
debt.

A few months passed. Then another accident
happened, this time involving his father. 'My father
ran over a young woman with his car,' Burro said.

'He injured his head badly and was not the same afterward.'

The young woman's parents demanded that the Burro family pay all her medical bills and additional money as compensation. The accident left his father in need of an operation; his father had to borrow 13,000 Lebanese pounds – the equivalent of $750 and a huge sum for his family – to pay medical bills. His father still needed a second operation for which there was no money. At the same time, the girl's family was pressing the family for money.

Burro said others then went to Abu Hassan and told him about the family's predicament. A few days later Abu Hassan sent a messenger to him, telling him to come to his office for a talk. The meeting was a carefully balanced combination of inducements and threats. Abu Hassan told him in detail about the financial situation of his father and how the problems could be resolved. According to Burro, Abu Hassan said: 'We are suggesting a suicide mission for you. What do you think about it? Remember, the future of your family is in your hands.'

Burro's first reaction to Abu Hassan's suggestion was to reject it. He had no interest in being a martyr, he said. At that point, Abu Hassan got tough. The youth was told that if he did not agree to the suicide mission, Abu Hassan would cause problems for his father and reopen the file on his motorcycle accident.

'I knew then and there that I would have no

choice but to say yes,' the youth said. 'I knew what
would happen if I said no.'

After a week and a half of thinking about little
else, Burro said, he returned to Abu Hassan's office
to give his answer. 'I told him, "OK, I accept a
suicide mission,"' he said. 'The reason I did was
financial incentives. It was not out of any ideology.'

After he had agreed to the suicide mission a very
pleased Abu Hassan told him, 'We will help your
father. We will finish with this problem. We will
help him. We will close the file on all of this, and
everything will be finished.'

But Abu Hassan apparently was concerned about
Burro's lack of religious convictions. He put Burro
in touch with some local Shi'a religious leaders to
instil in him some religious zeal. On 21 February
Abu Hassan came with another man, named Nour,
to inform Burro that his day had come. Nour was a
senior intelligence operative in the Amal security
apparatus. It was his job to arrange for the exploding car and to get it to the driver.

It is likely that these Amal security men had
links to intelligence agents from Syria or even Iran.
Syria has a variety of intelligence branches operating out of West Beirut, maintaining close contact
with the local militias and helping to coordinate
their anti-Israeli operations in southern Lebanon.

'They asked me if I was ready to go,' Burro said.
'I told them that I am not ready. I said, "No, no,
not today."'

Abu Hassan and Nour decided to give him until
the next day, apparently recognizing his nervous-

ness. The next day two cars set off from the Amal office for the trip to southern Lebanon. Burro rode in a Volvo with two men named Abu Ali and Khudur, whom he had not previously met. In the lead car, a Mazda, he said, were Nour and a man named Malik.

On the drive he was informed of his target. He was told to drive the suicide car at the Israeli military command headquarters for the western and central sectors of southern Lebanon, which was situated on a hill-top in a rundown former Lebanese Army barracks on the outskirts of Nabatiyeh. (About 100 Israeli soldiers worked at the headquarters before it was evacuated in the Israeli pullout from Nabatiyeh.)

If he could not reach the headquarters, Burro was to blow up the car next to an Israeli army convoy or patrol. 'They said the car would have 400 kilograms of TNT inside it,' Burro said, 'and that it would destroy all the homes and people in a radius of two square kilometres.

'I never saw the exploding car. I just heard them talking about it. They said there was a button on the left of the steering wheel and a button on the right. The one on the right was for operating and the one on the left for exploding. They had not given me any instructions about the car yet. I just heard Nour and Malik talking about it when we reached our destination. It was an American car.'

Most of the cars used for suicide bombings in Lebanon have had two buttons. One is pushed when the driver gets into the car, and it ensures the bomb will explode if the engine is turned off at any time. This guarantees that the driver will not back out at the last minute. The button on the left gives the driver the manual ability to detonate the bomb at the right time.

Other car bombs, such as the one used against the US Marines in 1983, are believed to have been detonated by a remote control radio signal by someone nearby so there would be no problems if the driver lost his nerve or was shot at.

In Zrariye, the group split up. Nour, Abu Ali and Khudur were to stay in Zrariye, while Malik and Burro were to drive together to Sir el Gharbiye, a small village farther inland. They arrived after dark. Malik told Burro to sleep there and that he would pick him up the next morning at 6.30. But the rendezvous did not take place.

Shortly after dawn the next morning, 23 February, the Israeli Army launched a search operation in Sir el Gharbiye, which is in the area of southern Lebanon from which they had withdrawn a few days earlier.

In their search of Sir el Gharbiye Israeli troops found a car rigged for a suicide bombing. This discovery led to interrogation of suspects and when it was found that Burro had arrived from Beirut the day before he became the prime suspect. He readily confessed. The *New York Times* reporter who interviewed him asked if he was angry that his mission had been foiled and wrote, 'Burro smiled broadly and said, "On the contrary, I feel great."'

Other missions were more successful. In March

1985 10 Israeli soldiers were killed in a suicide car bomb attack at the Lebanese border crossing point of Eggel. The driver rammed his explosives-laden car into an Israeli army lorry. The 'Islamic Resistance Front' claimed responsibility. Near Jezzine two other suicide car bomb attacks killed two Israeli soldiers and wounded seven others.

An interview on Damascus television, 17 August 1985, with a suicide bomber about to set out on a mission in southern Lebanon reveals something of the motives and outlook of the planners. The martyr-to-be was Abdullah Muhammad Khalid Abdul al-Qadir, a Syrian. The interview was shown after his death.

It began with an introduction by the presenter. 'An eagle from the Lebanese national resistance has recorded with his blood a new page of sacrifice and heroism in southern Lebanon . . . Before his martyrdom, hero martyr al-Qadir saluted Arab Syria and its leader, the symbol of Lebanese resistance, President Hafez Assad . . .'

The lengthy interview included these questions and answers:

Interviewer: In your opinion, what is the method by which we can expel the Zionist enemy from our Arab territory?

Al-Qadir: Our party and our leader Assad have taught us that peoples who struggle for their freedom and progress must triumph, that their struggle requires sacrifice so that they can teach lessons to the enemy . . . We are a sacrifice for our Arab nation in defence of our people. As struggler

President Hafez Assad has said, the best weapon with which we can face the enemies is the human being who insists on courting martyrdom.

Interviewer: Comrade, since you are from Syria what is the motive for your martyrdom on Lebanese territory?

Al-Qadir: It is out of my faith in the pan-Arab nature of the battle and the unity of the fate and destiny of the Arab nation. Even though I am from Syria, there is no difference for me if I perform my pan-Arab duty in any Arab spot, be it Syria, Lebanon or Palestine. This is because the enemy is not against Lebanon alone or Syria alone. This is what our leader Hafez Assad taught us.

The posthumous interview is interesting. The fact that it was carried on state-controlled Syrian television indicates an official endorsement of the suicide bombings.

Towards the end of 1985 the jihad planners in Beirut and Baalbek realized that suicide bombing was becoming unproductive; in a period of three months it had caused no damage. Some attackers, on the way to hit a target, were fired at by soldiers of the South Lebanon Army and died when their vehicles blew up. By November 1985 even the Lebanese press was putting the 'martyrs of the resistance' on the lower half of the front page.

At this point somebody thought of donkey and mule bombers. On at least three occasions girls leading or riding donkeys carrying heavy loads of explosives were intercepted in southern Lebanon during late 1985. Ma'ila Safanji, aged 17, from the village of Kahmed a-Luz near Lake Karoun, was spotted by South Lebanon Army soldiers when she and two men tried to take a mule-bomb into a security zone. The three terrorists were also carrying large quantities of explosives. The soldiers opened fire, blowing up the mule and the men and wounding the girl in the leg. She was treated in hospital and returned to her village.

Ma'ila Safanji and her companions may not have intended to blow themselves up but in mid-October holy war body-bombers attacked Voice of Hope radio and television station near Khiam in southern Lebanon. Voice of Hope was a natural target for Islamic Jihad if only because it was broadcasting readings from the *Bible*. The American evangelist, George Otis, had founded Voice of Hope in 1975 as a way of passing messages between members of families separated by the terrorist wars which had raged for years in southern Lebanon. On 17 October 1985 holy war warriors with more than 200 lb of explosives strapped to their backs killed a guard outside the entrance to the broadcasting station and rushed in. With a battery press button they set off the charge which blew up the building and killed them. Should they have changed their minds about suicide a number of terrorists who had taken up positions nearby would have set off the explosives by rifle fire.

Islamic Jihad's bombing tactics evolved at Melli University, Iran, from a study of operations carried out by the Irish Republican Army and the Palestine

Liberation Organization. Both these groups had
had much experience and the Islamic Jihad leaders
tapped it. They noted that the IRA had been
spectacularly successful in blowing up police and
army vehicles by remote controlled explosions; the
PLO had perfected the technique of the bomb
concealed in some 'innocent' object. Islamic Jihad's
researchers were particularly impressed by the
success of the refrigerator bomb which killed scores
of people in Zion Square, Jerusalem and in the
PLO tactic of placing bombs in melons and pine-
apples and leaving them in public markets.

PLO bomb experts were invited to training
schools in Iran and Lebanon to demonstrate their
techniques. The IRA was also invited to send
instructors but declined so Islamic Jihad sent a
small group of Iranians and Lebanese to Ireland
where they were given lessons in rigging cars with
bombs to be set off electronically at a safe distance.

Bombs are seen as cost-effective because a few
men can cause death and destruction out of all
proportion to their own number. Islamic Jihad and
its many offshoots and associates prefer bombs but
their leaders acknowledge that at times attackers
with firearms 'create a better impact.'

When I visited a PLO terrorist training camp at
Ein el Hilwe, southern Lebanon, in the mid-1970s
an instructor told me, 'Killing with bombs is effective but it is also too indiscriminate for the real
terror which is our aim. It is better for a small
group of commandos to seize an aircraft or a
roomful of people and kill two or three over a

period. The survivors never forget the experience
– and we do not want them to forget.'

Islamic Jihad has learnt this lesson and has
developed some tactics of its own. One of them is
that of 'anticipation of attack,' supposedly presented to the jihad high command by Hussein
Moussawi of Islamic Amal. It is simply a matter of
giving repeated warnings and threats, using different voices, that bomb attacks will be made against
certain, named targets. The aim is to unnerve the
staff and guards of the place threatened. Generally
the place *is* attacked but this may take place months
after the first threat, by which time the staff,
according to Islamic Jihad thinking, will be
demoralized.

After the American embassy bombing in September 1983 the US Assistant Secretary of State
Richard Murphy flew to Beirut. 'The Muslim killers have failed in their goal of sapping the political
will of the US government,' he said. 'They always
will.'

However, the American withdrawal from Beirut
after the massacre of the Marines proved, at least
to Islamic Jihad, that American will can be broken.
The leaders plan to use kamikaze suicide aircraft
bombers and their time cannot be far off.

CHAPTER ELEVEN

Communiqués from the war fronts:
Africa

Jihad in Africa has shown itself in several forms. For instance, open warfare and introduction of the Shari'a law in Sudan; conversion of Christians to Islam in West African states; empire-building by Libya in Chad, Malta, Burkino Faso and elsewhere; threats of war, also by Libya, against Egypt, Tunisia and Algeria; fundamentalist violence in Tunisia and Morocco.

SUDAN

Sudan has been caught up in jihad since the days of the famous Muhammad Ahmad ibn Abdullah, the Mahdi, who founded what could be called the first Islamic state of modern times. He died in 1885, five months after his forces had crushed those of General Gordon in Khartoum, but his state lasted 13 years under his chosen successor, the Khalifa Abdullah. It was then destroyed by the British army of General Kitchener.

Mahdism survived through the shrewdness of the Mahdi's son, Abdul Rahman, who led the Ansar – the name given to the Mahdi's followers – and taught them that jihad could succeed through political means. To this end he co-operated with the British during World War 1 and was knighted by George V.

Following Abdul Rahman's death in 1959 a split occurred in the Ansar/Mahdist party. When Gafaar Nimeiri came to power in a coup in 1969 he arrested Sadiq, Abdul Rahman's grandson, and held him without trial. Nimeiri was so fearful of the Mahdists that in 1970, in the name of holy war, he set out to annihilate them. He was supported by President Nasser of Egypt who sent aircraft under the command of Husni Mubarak, then commander of the Egyptian air force, to bomb and strafe Aba Island in the White Nile; the original Mahdi had launched his movement from the island, which remained the main centre of Mahdism. At least 20,000 Mahdists were killed though some estimates go as high as 50,000. The Imam Al-Hadi, a senior leader, trying to flee to Ethiopia was caught and murdered. Mahdism was declared subversive and proscribed and suppressed. This was jihad with a vengeance, justified by Nimeiri as essential for the good of the Sudanese people. But Mahdism itself is a jihad movement and it is still a force to be reckoned with.

After Nimeiri seized power the Soviet Union was quick to give him military aid and in support of Nimeiri's holy war against the Christians in the southern part of the country Soviet bombers attacked the Christian guerrilla army.

The war formally ended in 1972 but Islamic oppression from the north forced the Christians to continue guerrilla activity through their Sudan People's Liberation Army. Its leader, John Garang, found allies in Ethiopia and Libya, both of which wanted to undermine the Nimeiri government. That Gaddafi, an Islamic fanatic, should help Garang, a Christian, might seem strange but Gaddafi's assistance was consistent with *Koranic* holy war teaching that a temporary alliance with Christians is permissible if the end is important enough. Gaddafi wanted to break Sudan's ties with Egypt, one of his main enemies. He planned to 'deal with' Garang once he had taken over Sudan with Libyan troops. Garang had little chance of attaining power in Sudan, with or without Gaddafi's help, because Muslims outnumber Christians four to one. Realistically, this 'Tsar of the South', as he is called, could hope for no more than to become president of a new Christian state formed from southern Sudan.

On 5 April 1985 Nimeiri was overthrown in a military coup led by General Swaw al-Dhahab. This made no difference to the civil war, in which Garang was consistently successful. Government casualties mounted throughout 1985 and the army became demoralized. The army leaders are reluctant to allow the south to secede; in an area the size of France it contains Sudan's most promising oil fields.

Nimeiri had not merely waged a jihad against his own Christians but had imposed Shari'a law nationwide. Encouraged by Saudi Arabia in particular but also by emissaries from Iran, he brought in all the harsh punishments of Islamic law; even 'contemplation of adultery' became a capital offence. On Fridays offenders were taken to the great stadium of Khartoum where thousands gathered to watch the punishments – flogging, amputation and hanging – inflicted.

The most controversial execution was that of Mahmud Muhammad Taha, aged 76, the leader of the Republican Brothers. A devout Muslim, Taha subscribed to the two parts of the *Shahada*, or confession of faith: 'There is no God but God and Muhammad is his prophet.' Yet he was accused of 'heresy', which in Islam means denying or subtracting from that essential declaration. All sorts of additions have been made to it by different Muslim groups – by Shi'as, Ismailis, Bhoras and Sufi mystics, both Shi'a and Sunni. Their enlarged doctrines have not been denounced as heresies.

Taha had been openly teaching his own views for 40 years and he led a community no more than 700-strong. However, they were enthusiastic pamphleteers and they influenced the Sudanese educated governing class. Taha particularly annoyed President Nimeiri by arguing that no Muslim state should carry the title 'Islamic': it was not necessary and its use demeaned the religion. According to Taha, an ideal Muslim state should be governed by a presidential system with the president elected by an elected parliament, both with a fixed term of four years. He also believed in the equality of men and women and advocated monogamy.

Orthodox Islamic establishments hate this open-minded fresh approach. Nimeiri announced that Taha was hanged because he opposed Sudan's policy of punishing criminals by amputation and flogging. However, Taha was known to accept

these punishments; he believed literally in an eye
for an eye. What he objected to was their summary
application by Sudan's special courts. His own trial
was summary and swift. Many writers and lawyers
throughout the Arab world denounced Taha's hanging. However, Saudi Arabia gave prominence to
the prosecution case against Taha and newspaper
editorials supported the sentence.

Nimeiri's aim was to 'purify' his people and thus
win a reputation within Islam as a great leader; his
country was virtually bankrupt and he needed
money from the bottomless coffers of Saudi Arabia
– but this would not be forthcoming unless he
proved himself to be truly Islamic.

After Nimeiri was overthrown in 1985 the sever-
ity of Shari'a punishments was relaxed, partly
through the efforts of Sudan's professional classes
but equally through pressure from the United
States, which was contributing as much money to
Sudan as Saudi Arabia.

Gaddafi's activities in Sudan continued. During
torrential rains in September 1985 when Western
aid trucks were unable to get through mud to
deliver food to western Sudan, Libya sent a convoy
of 43 trucks and tracked vehicles from Benghazi to
El Fasher in Darfur Province in two weeks. This
was a remarkable feat – but under the food lay
arms and ammunition for a people's holy war
uprising. Without entering El Fasher an escort of
several hundred Libyan troops disappeared into
the Sudanese wilderness to distribute the weapons
and supplies to pro-Libyan guerrillas.

NIGERIA

Fundamentalism of an extreme kind developed in
Nigeria in 1980, largely as a result of help and
encouragement from Colonel Gaddafi. The founder
of a holy war sect, Muhammad Marwa, came from
Cameroon and settled in Nigeria where he became
known to his followers as the Maitatsine or
prophet, similar to the Mahdi or 'expected one'
known to the Muslims of Sudan in the 19th
century.

In 1980, in Kano, Marwa and his followers rose
in rebellion against the state and during the fighting 4,000 people were killed. Marwa himself, who
believed that Nigeria should declare itself an
Islamic state, was killed. In 1982 other riots took
place in the north-eastern town of Maiduguri, and
800 people died. In northern Nigeria in 1984 a
fresh wave of violence swept the region, and again
in April and May 1985.

This violence was a prelude to events in February 1986 when the Nigerian government decided
to join the Islamic Conference Organization (ICO).
This, in effect, was a declaration that the nation
itself is Islamic. Every Islamic country formally
congratulated the Nigerian government on its
decision but several went much further. Saudi
Arabia instantly announced 'generous' financial aid
while Iran and Libya offered 'special' military
instructors. 'Special' meant, by the standards of
Gaddafi and Khomeini, war-minded ayatollahs
skilled in the preaching and teaching of jihad.

In fact, Libyan and Iranian clerical emissaries

had been in Muslim Nigeria for some years,
reminding Muslims of the splendours of the empire
of Shehu Usman dan Fodio, Commander of the
Faithful. In Fodio's time, in the early 19th century,
Fodio's armies, in the name of Allah, swept aside
all opposition. The learned foreign ayatollahs have
been preaching that these great times can come
again to the region, but only if it is controlled by
Muslims.

Islam is undoubtedly the dominant presence in
Africa's most populous country. But for the moment
the military men in control are drawn from all the
regions; some are Christians from the south. In
1986 the challenge facing them and the powerful
Christian minority was to defuse the furore caused
by the government's decision to join the ICO
without seeming to dislike or distrust Muslim ways
of life and Muslim festivals, such as the sallah, the
great quasi-martial celebration which follows the
end of the fasting month of Ramadan.

The nationalistic and realistic Christians know
that faith in the old traditions, whether Muslim or
Christian, is a strong source of stability. But they
recognize that Islam in its more moderate form is
under threat in Nigeria and all Africa from infiltration across the desert by the fanatics of Iran, Libya
and Lebanon.

RWANDA

In May 1985 Colonel Gaddafi, during a speech in
Kigali, capital of Rwanda, declared holy war against

Christianity in black Africa and accused the Christian Church of being 'false, infidel and irreligious.' 'Africa must be Muslim,' Gaddafi said. 'Christians are intruders in Africa and are agents of colonialism. We must wage a holy war so that Islam will spread in Africa.'[1]

The occasion for his attack on Christianity was the opening of a mosque and an Islamic centre, worth $5 million, jointly financed by Libya and the United Arab Emirates. Standing with Gaddafi as he made his challenging speech was the Rwandan president, Juvenal Habyarimana, who in 1984 had renounced his Christian beliefs and turned to Islam.

'The Islamic revolution stems from Libya,' Gaddafi said, 'and the international Islamic call has emerged from Libya. You Rwandans must consider Libya your first country and must rely on your Muslim brothers in Libya. We are ready to share everything with you.'

Establishment of the Kigali centre was a considerable holy war coup for Gaddafi, as he made clear in part of his speech. 'You are hoisting the banner of Islam below the equator, in the heart of Africa, and declaring that Muhammad is the messiah of Allah. You are facing up to the challenge of the Christian Church, which does not recognize the prophecy of Muhammad. You must encourage the children of Christians to embrace Islam and

[1] The speech was broadcast in Arabic the same day over *The Voice of the Greater Arab Homeland* from Tripoli: 17 May 2015 GMT.

teach them that Christianity is not the religion of Africans.'

He accused Christianity of being 'the religion of colonialism and the religion of the French, Belgian, German and American enemies.' At another point in his long speech he called Christianity the 'religion of the Jews.' Urging the Rwandans to co-operate with their Muslim brothers in Burundi, Zaire and Uganda, Gaddafi asked them to send missionaries to these countries to combat the 'evil activities' of Christian missionaries.

Fiercely attacking President Mobutu of Zaire, he said it was the duty of every Muslim to kill Mobutu and his associates. 'You must incite Muslims in Zaire and urge them to engage in jihad so that Mobutu may be overthrown. He who kills this man will go to Paradise.'

In another section of his speech Gaddafi told his Rwandan audience, 'The first step for you is to teach your children Islam and the Arabic language; then idolaters must be converted to Islam. Then there must be an attempt to introduce the children of Christians to Islam so that they will not grow up to be Christians just because their parents were Christians. From this year you must start having contact with Muslims in the neighbouring countries so that Muslims may protect one another. Allah wants you to fight in one rank and who does not do so is outside Islam and Allah will not let him enter Paradise.'

Gaddafi assured the Rwandans that not only Libya and the United Arab Emirates were behind

them but the entire Arab homeland. He promised
to build mosques and Islamic centres 'everywhere'
in the struggle against Christianity; the struggle
would continue day and night until Islam
triumphed over Christianity in Africa. He concluded his speech with a rhetorical exhortation as
his audience prostrated themselves before him:
'Muslims, here there will be glory and eternal life
because you are spreading Islam throughout Africa
beyond the equator. You will be rewarded and you
will go to Paradise because you are spreading
Islam.'

CHAD

Within months of Colonel Gaddafi's coup against
the Libyan monarchy in September 1969 he began
to intervene in the factional war then afflicting
Chad. When overthrowing King Idris, Gaddafi had
declared jihad on the ground that monarchs were
'anathema to Allah and Islam'. Now he called for
jihad in Chad to 'remove the imperialist French.'
Formerly part of French equatorial Africa, Chad
had become independent in 1960 but the three
northernmost provinces remained under French
military administration until 1965. By the time
Gaddafi declared holy war the French had already
gone although it was understood that they would
return and would send a peace-keeping force
should this be necessary.

In 1973 Libya occupied the Aozou Strip, a 60-
mile-wide stretch of mountainous desert in the
north. Using this as a base Gaddafi frustrated

attempts to produce a stable and independent
government in Chad; he supported Goukouni
Oeddai against Hisseine Habŕe and fomented
trouble in the Christian south against Habŕe.
Renewing his jihad call in 1980, with the encouragement of Ayatollah Khomeini, Gaddafi sent a
tank force into Libya and built a large airbase north
of the capital, Ndjamena.

Despite efforts by the Organization of African
Unity to induce Gaddafi to withdraw his troops
Libyan aggression continued into 1973, with Gaddafi demanding a declaration of Chad's 'Arabness'
– although Arabs are in the minority in Chad – and
close integration with Libya. Zaire and France sent
troops and both countries announced that their
forces would not leave Chad while Libyan troops
remained. After tortuous diplomacy, in September
1984 Mitterand and Gaddafi met in Cyprus and
signed an agreement that both would withdraw
their troops simultaneously. The French kept the
treaty; the Libyans did not. Once again, Gaddafi
was keeping faith with the *Koran* which permits
truces and treaties with infidels for the purpose of
gaining some advantage. His troops were still in
Chad in 1988.

LIBYA
As I have explained elsewhere Colonel Gaddafi of
Libya is one of the field marshals of jihad. However, he is more than a fundamentalist advocate of
holy war; he is also a chaotic mixture of Arab
nationalist, anarchist and Marxist. His *Green Book*
promoted the idea of 'direct democracy' on the

anarchist model; this meant the abolition of political parties and the state bureaucracy which were replaced by 'people's committees' and syndicates. This development, together with Gaddafi's novel ideas on economics, has produced a new and ruthless type of state bureaucracy controlled by Gaddafi as dictator.

Gaddafi's activities are even wider than those of the Iranian ayatollahs or the PLO, with both of whom Gaddafi is in alliance. At various times since 1969 Gaddafi has declared holy war against the West, Christendom, the Catholic Church, Britain, the United States, Spain, France, Italy, Egypt, Israel, Sudan, Tunisia, Morocco, all the Arab monarchs – as a group and individually – 'Zionists,' Libyan dissidents, President Marcos of the Philippines, President Saddam Hussein of Iraq, President Mitterand of France, Prime Minister Thatcher of Britain, President Reagan of the United States and other states, organizations and individual leaders.

At the same time he has declared his support for the Irish Republican Army, the Palestine Liberation Organization and the various factions which make up the PLO, the anti-Marcos guerrillas of the Philippines, the Black Panthers of the US, and most of the terrorist organizations of Western Europe.

Occasionally he has cancelled or deferred jihad. For instance, after years of supporting the Polisario guerrilla fighters of Western Sahara against King Hassan II of Morocco he signed a treaty of peace and co-operation with Hassan. His main reason for doing this was to induce Hassan to return to Libya an opponent of the Gaddafi regime, Omar Muhayshi.[2] Muhayshi, a boyhood friend of Gaddafi, became a high-ranking official in the revolutionary regime but in 1974 he turned against Gaddafi when it was clear that he was wasting Libya's oil wealth on a dream of becoming leader of the Arab world. His brutality and support for terrorism also disillusioned Muhayshi, who joined the opposition.

A plot to overthrow Gaddafi – he calls it the 'Muhayshi plot' – was aborted and the conspirators went into hiding. Most were rounded up and executed in March 1976. Muhayshi, having been welcomed to Morocco, published revealing memoirs of Gaddafi and criticized him in radio programmes from Egypt and Tunisia.

For eight years Gaddafi tried to have his former friend murdered; he even offered a former CIA agent $1 million to arrange a killing. Finally, he offered to cut off Libyan aid to the Polisario guerrillas fighting King Hassan in Western Sahara if Hassan would betray Muhayshi. In 1984 friends warned Muhayshi that he was part of the treaty deal but he trusted the king. It is not clear whether Libyan agents were allowed to kidnap him in Morocco or whether the king's men put him on a plane for Tripoli. Gaddafi and a death squad were

---

[2] I photographed Muhayshi when visiting Libya in 1972; a tall alert looking man, he seemed to me at the time to be the most intelligent of the 12 men who made up the Revolutionary Council.

waiting at the foot of the boarding stairs. Here the 'arch traitor' was stomped to death.

Muhayshi was only one of 50,000 dissidents who have chosen to live outside Libya. All are potential targets for holy war retribution. Hit teams have killed victims in several European countries. Many other expatriate Libyans were the subjects of attempted murders. Early in 1985 Gaddafi created what became known to the Libyan opposition as 'suicide incubators' to train volunteers to exterminate the Libyan enemies of the regime. The term suicide martyrs is inappropriate because the Libyans, unlike Iranians, Lebanese Shi'as and some Palestinians, are not the stuff of which suicide attackers are made. In any case, they seemed able to achieve their ends without committing suicide. A group calling itself al-Borkan, the volcano, claimed responsibility for various murders, including that of Ammar al Tagazzy, a former Libyan ambassador to Italy. In mid-1985, according to Western intelligence agencies, about 120 Libyan hit squads were at large outside Libya.

A special 'revolutionary duty group', the Mutaresbesoun, was trained for operations in Britain. Its members were young men, with some women, who had studied in Europe and the US. Many spoke flawless English and could pass in appearance for English. At that time Gaddafi remained angry with Britain for having broken off diplomatic relations after the St James Square siege. As the government would not re-establish relations, he said that he was no longer obliged to 'hold back the holy impulse of true Libyans to eliminate our enemies.' *The Sunday Times* infiltrated a meeting of 100 pro-Gaddafi students in London and reported that 'they worked themselves into a revolutionary frenzy, repeatedly chanting "Revolution is in our hearts; we would rather die than sacrifice it."'

Deployment of these squads was in keeping with Gaddafi's declaration in April 1984 of 'sacred action' – another term for holy war against dissident Libyans living abroad – especially those in Britain, West Germany and the United States. In a speech to the Libyan People's Congress, Gaddafi said: 'It is legitimate for our entire people to liquidate its enemies abroad and quite openly.' Within days a Libyan opponent of the regime was shot dead in Bonn and two Germans passing by were seriously hurt.

Within Libya Gaddafi depends for his survival on loyal tribal troops and many hundreds of East German security guards. Part of his entourage, especially when he travels abroad, is a group of young women in combat dress. Dubbed by Western journalists as the 'Green Nuns' because of their appearance, these girls are supposed to have dedicated their lives to Gaddafi's jihad.

Gaddafi had set up terrorist training schools for various factions of the PLO within a year of his coming to power in 1969. Quite soon these schools were available to terrorists from almost every part of the world, provided that its leaders professed to be supporters of Gaddafi and his causes. In 1982 he established his 'Martyrs classes' – the 'incuba-tors' for Islamic volunteers.

Gaddafi called the young people at these schools the Generation of Wrath and he profoundly influenced them with his prophetic relevations and 'inspired insight' – his term – based as much on his own *Green Book* as on the *Koran*. Their training was rigorous intellectually, emotionally and militarily and at the end of it was the prospect of holy war. Each college and school had three directors, responsible respectively for ideology, military training and academic subjects. Not all students were expected to become martyrs but all were expected to apply for this honour. The greatest honour would go to the martyr who blew up the 'Black House', that is, Washington's White House.

The ideological director and his staff taught that the United States was a 'terrorist state' and must therefore, as a matter of simple human justice and Islamic duty, be punished. But the US was not the only offender. According to Gaddafi's Third Universal Theory rulers everywhere must be either deposed or killed, Arab as well as Western and Communist leaders, so that 'power could devolve to the people.'

In Libya the conventional or regular army was on the way out and being replaced by 'people under arms.' By 1982 Gaddafi had turned Libya into one of the world's most militarized and militaristic nations. Every child, male and female, started basic military training at the age of 14 with the handling of light arms. By the time Libyans graduated from secondary school or university they were specialists in one field or another of warfare. Women had 'equal military rights' with men; Libya might well be the only Arab country with women fighter pilots.

The purpose of having a 'people under arms' was supposed to eliminate the possibility of coup d'état and military adventurism – though all of Gaddafi's neighbours in Africa considered him to be the most dangerous of military adventurers. No citizen could serve in the army for more than a period each year so that, in line with the Third Universal Theory, it would not be possible for any over ambitious man to build up a following from among the armed forces. All direction was to come from committees and congresses, which changed their members frequently so that nobody became too powerful.

In July 1985 Gaddafi declared an unprecedented form of jihad against the Hajj or pilgrimage to Mecca. Libyan pilgrims, he announced, would no longer be allowed to visit the grave of the Prophet Muhammad when fulfilling the Hajj rites; they were also forbidden to visit Medina. New regulations stipulated that pilgrims would in future be divided into groups of no more than 10 people, each of them headed by a member of Gaddafi's revolutionary committees. This was to prevent any Libyan pilgrim from seeking asylum in Gulf countries and also from visiting the Prophet's tomb.

In fact, the Hajj had become the occasion and the tomb the place where the opposition National Front for the Salvation of Libya (NFSL) and other

بِسْمِ ٱللَّهِ ٱلرَّحْمَٰنِ ٱلرَّحِيمِ

The Arabic invocation which accompanies almost everything that is
written or said within Islam. It means 'In the name of Allah, the
merciful, the compassionate'. Ayatollah Khomeini uses this
language when calling for death to his enemies. Islamic Jihad terror
squads and spokesmen use it to preface each announcement they
might make about some act of holy war.

وَلَن يَجْعَلَ ٱللَّهُ لِلْكَٰفِرِينَ عَلَى ٱلْمُؤْمِنِينَ سَبِيلًا ﴿١٤١﴾

'And Allah will never grant to the unbelievers a way (to triumph)
over the believers.' Koran, iv, 141. This is one of the major sayings
on which the Islamic holy war leaders base their claims to
supremacy over Christians, Jews and those Muslims who oppose
them.

LEFT: Leila Khaled, the first famous Arab woman terrorist of modern times. At this rally in Beirut in 1970 she was preaching holy war.

BELOW: President Hafez Assad of Syria (hands on hips) inspecting fortifications on the Golan Heights. Next to him is the Defence Minister, Mustafa Tlaas and on Tlass' left is General Rifaat Assad, the President's brother. President Assad is a close ally and supporter of Ayatollah Khomeini and of Colonel Gaddafi. With them he is one of the principal backers of Islamic Jihad.

Syrian girl soldiers, members of the 500,000-strong army, during training for holy war.

President Gaddafi of Libya in 1973 issued a poster showing his claim to be the leader of the entire Arab world; the Arabic slogan across it reads 'One Arab motherland'. He presented a copy, in a silver frame, to the author. His advisers induced him to withdraw and destroy the poster because it was bound to anger other Arab nations; they might not want to be ruled by Gaddafi. This was Gaddafi's first declaration of holy war, as the 'Mahdi' or messiah of the Arab nation, after he came to power in 1969.

An American victim of Islamic Jihad. This American marine was one of the 241 marines killed in Beirut when a suicide car-bomber blew up their base. The photograph was taken a few days before the attack.

Yasser Arafat, attending a passing out parade of very young terrorists, calls for Allah's blessing on a 'gunman' aged 10.

LEFT: An 'illegal photograph' of preparations for an execution in Iran. The victim was found guilty by a Revolutionary Court of crimes against Allah's representative – Ayatollah Khomeini.

BELOW: In their Holy War against the invading Russians the Afghan warriors rarely have a chance to capture a tank. Here they give praise to Allah for their victory.

A poster produced by the 'Cultural Arts Section' of the Palestine
Liberation Organisation. The fedayeen are the guerrilla martyrs.

opposition groups meet Libyan citizens and recruit them. Gaddafi was well aware of this. In 1983, 1984 and 1985 he sent revolutionary committee-men to Mecca to counter opposition propaganda. Shortly before Hajj time in 1984 he told the revolutionary committees, 'Go to the Hajj and whenever you meet the stray dogs [opponents], kill them.' Saudi Arabian guards at the holy places seized a quantity of arms from Libyans.

In 1986 Gaddafi launched his 'International People's Front' and in newspaper advertisements in several languages called for volunteers to join the Front, which is intended to be a mercenary army of grand proportions. Gaddafi sees it as a holy war army which will fight 'all the forces of aggression.' One of the first paid advertisements in English appeared in the Maltese daily newspaper, *l'oriz-zont – Il-Gimgha* on 21 February 1986. Some of the phraseology is a little difficult to follow but it is worth quoting in full as possibly the first attempt by a nation, in modern times, to raise an army in such a way.

A CALL FOR JOINING THE LIBYAN ARAB ARMED FORCES
Peoples unite and Liberate

Strugglers, oppressed and Muslims worldwide – unite and you will open up the gates for a new society – one of freedom, happiness and prosperity. Brothers in all societies under oppression, tyranny and exploitation.

Socialist People's Libyan Arab Jamahiriya,[3] the First

---

[3] The Arab word means 'the state of the masses.'

Jamahiriya in history heralding the next international Revolution has announced the International People's Front that struggles for the toppling all types of dictatorial governments and demolishing all forms of Man's exploitation of Man.

We are all being called upon to contribute in establishing and developing this front to reinforce the struggle of Socialist People's Libyan Arab Jamahiriya against Imperialism, US aggression and the provocations coupled with terrorism aiming at intimidating our struggling people and wrecking our Socialist People's advancement let alone compelling it to stop supporting the oppressed peoples and world liberation movement as well as preventing it from backing all the humanitarian efforts it exerts that fight Imperialism, Zionism, Racism and Fascism.

We, the masses all over the world, hold that it is our duty to contribute in backing the strenous efforts exerted by Socialist People's Libyan Arab Jamahiriya.

The Great International Revolutionary, Muammar Al Qathafi, Leader of the Great Al Fateh Revolution has announced that the doors are now open for volunteers to establish the first armed people of Socialist People's Libyan Arab Jamahiriya – The first Jamahiriya in History – the First State of masses. Now volunteers are welcome to work in technical and installation fields in all types of weapons the Naval, air and land ones as well as air defence for all citizens from the world at large.

Our contribution in the work in these fields will strengthen and back the efforts exerted to fight Imperialism everywhere, fight as well as the efforts made to strengthen and advance the first Jamahiriya in the world.

The forces of aggression and exploitation come in troops to foil such remarkable human achievement so as not to be followed suit worldwide to dismantle once and for all the forms of exploitation and hegemony throughout the world.

They, the oppressors, make every endeavours to prevent you from taking your road for freedom, happiness and prosperity and for building the new society – the one of justice, equality, security and peace.

We, the defenders of freedom, the enemies of Imperialism and all forms of aggression against peoples and who want to defend our humanity after being trampled down by the dictatorial and fascist forces, must join the first International People's army that is set on fighting the forces of evil, for they aim at wrecking man's peace on our globe.

Socialist People's Libyan Arab Jamahiriya has announced its call for all freedom-fighters and struggles for all the Nations worldwide to be like-wise officers, non-commissioned officers and soldiers with the armed People and that they will have the same rights and duties of the Libyan Arab people.

See you soon under the First Flag of Jamahiriya.

Victory to our Cause – that of Humanity.

Proceed and the Revolutionary struggle continues.

TUNISIA

Beginning on 6 August 1985 Libya began to expel many of its 90,000 Tunisian workers and within six days 20,000 had been forced out. The expulsions were really deportations because the Tunisians (as well as many Egyptians) were not allowed to take money or possessions with them; even their passports were confiscated.

The probable immediate reason for the expulsion was that Tunisia had uncovered a Libyan holy war espionage network and following this, Bechi Essid, the pro-Libyan leader of the Arab Nationalist Rally, was imprisoned. Tunisia has also incurred Gaddafi's anger because of the government's close relationship with the US. He gave his Tunisian guestworkers the chance of remaining in Libya if they agreed to become Libyan citizens.

The return of large numbers of Tunisians to their own country create enormous economic, social and security problems for the government. The economic problems in particular forced Tunisia to move closer politically to Algeria, which it did not want to do as it prizes its independence.

MOROCCO

Following the treaty signed between Libya and Morocco in 1984 King Hassan expected Libyan intrigue against him to be stopped. Instead it has continued and is constantly aided and abetted by the many Iranian agents, including high-ranking ayatollahs, who have been sent to Morocco to bring about the monarchy's downfall.

For Islamic Jihad Hassan is guilty of three major crimes. He is a monarch; he permits the 'Great Satan' United States to have military bases in Morocco; and he refuses to discuss government policy with the religious hierarchy.

For the Islamic Jihad planners Morocco is of great historical and strategic importance. It was from Morocco that Islam in its early years made its great advances into Western Europe. Muslims captured and colonized much of Spain and held it against repeated attacks for eight centuries. Muslim historians date the beginning of Islam's imperial decline from 25 November 1491 when Abdullah, the last king of Granada, surrendered the city to Christian forces. From that time Islam retreated back to Africa. Islamic Jihad's longer term strategy is to recover Spain and restore history to its 'correct course.' The jumping off point for this 'invasion' is Morocco, which must first itself be revolutionized. Between 1975 and 1987 King Hassan survived 12 known assassination attempts, at least half of which were inspired by fundamentalist conspirators. Hassan himself has never directly declared jihad, even against the Polisario guerrillas of Western Sahara who want independence from Morocco. However, his ministers have been constrained at various Islamic conferences to join in general declarations of holy war.

EGYPT
See Chapter Two.

CHAPTER TWELVE

Communiqués from the war fronts:
Asia, Africa

AFGHANISTAN

When the Soviet Union invaded Afghanistan in December 1979 it was inevitable that the Islamic world would declare jihad in response. There was some apparent contradiction in this considering that the Afghanistan government, under the Soviet puppet president Babrak Kamal, ordered the Afghan army to co-operate with the Soviet army.

The call for holy war came from the Afghan hill tribes, the mujahideen – a fiercely Islamic people who saw their faith and liberty threatened by the atheist Soviet invaders. Because the mujahideen receive a continuous supply of weapons from certain Muslim countries – notably Egypt, Saudi Arabia and Pakistan – they have been able to put up a much stiffer resistance than the Soviet high command had considered possible. However, there is no doubt that the spirit of jihad, fostered by the Afghan mullahs, gives the mujahideen resistance movement its sharp edge.

At the beginning of the war the Russian soldiers could see no reason to fight. The resistance reported at that time that the soldiers chose to fire in the air rather than obey orders to shoot villagers. But the mujahideen, increasingly under the influence of extremist mullahs, tortured captured Russians before killing them. Mutilated bodies were left on roads and tracks to be found by horrified comrades. It became common for Russian officers in particular to shoot themselves when in imminent danger of being captured by the mujahideen. Mutilation and torture of prisoners has been common throughout the history of holy war, though it is not sanctioned by the *Koran*.

Pakistan, with claims or pretensions to be the leader of Islam – on the grounds of its political importance, possession of the 'Islamic bomb', large size of population – felt obliged to give refuge to Afghan refugees and to arm and supply the mujahideen. Soviet military threats against Pakistan and its diplomatic appeals not to supply the rebellious Afghan tribesmen meant nothing in the face of the Islamic affinity which binds Pakistan to the mujahideen. General Zia al-Huq, Pakistan's leader, made it clear that Babrak Kamal's Kabul government had betrayed Islam in aligning itself with the Russians. While not itself involved in a declared jihad, Pakistan considers that it is supporting legitimate holy war.

Afghans who die fighting the Soviet army are considered martyrs, just as surely as any Arab or Iranian killed while attacking the 'Great Satan' and its allies. When a guerrilla is killed the local commander pronounces him to be a shaheed (martyr) and his comrades offer a short prayer. They try to delay the burial until there is time for them to recite the whole of the *Koran*; on occasions the text will be broken into as many as 30 parts and

30 men will intone the sections together. When a man dies without suffering, through the impact of bullets or bomb fragments, he is buried in his clothes; this is considered the most honourable way to be buried. A man who is not killed instantly but is given treatment before death has his body undressed, washed and wrapped in a white sheet for burial.

Short of annihilating every man, woman and child of the hill and mountain communities the Soviet armies could never subjugate the mujahideen, whose mullahs will see to it that the fighting spirit which emanates from jihad remains undiminished.

BANGLADESH

For half a century before the partition of India and Pakistan in 1948 the British ruled the Chittagong Hill Tracts in an enlightened way. The inhabitants of the area were nearly all Buddhists, from 12 different tribes, with Chakma people predominating. On partition the Hill Tracts and their Buddhists were handed over to Pakistan, a martial, theocratic society, rather than to democratic, secular India. The decision was to prove disastrous.

In 1951 there were 10 Buddhists to every Bengali Muslim. With the founding of Bangladesh in 1971 the Chakmas came under systematic attack when the new government decided to settle the Hill Tracts with Muslim/Bengalis from the crowded river plains of the Ganges and Brahmaputra. More than 200,000 Bengalis were settled in Chakma country without Chakma consent.

Though without a martial tradition, the Chakmas created a self-defence force in 1974. At that point the Bangladeshi Muslim government declared jihad against the Buddhists. Unable to break the Chakmas in a 10-year conflict the army in 1984 sent the crack 24th Division, the 'Bengal Tigers,' into the Hill Tracts with orders to 'solve the Chakma problem.'

Much influenced by visiting Iranian and Lebanese Shi'as, the government has been ruthless. Survival International estimates that by the end of 1985 185,000 Buddhists had died in a campaign of genocide. Up to 15,000 had been detained without trial and many had been tortured. Bengali Muslims, by 1985, made up 50 per cent of the population.

Being peace-loving people, the Buddhists of the Chittagong tracts have no concept similar to holy war but their relatively few guerrillas, who are supplied by the Soviet Union, have become expert fighters. The war could continue for another 10 years – or until the Bangladeshi government achieves its aim of genocide.

PAKISTAN

In an academic and theoretical way, Pakistan is the base Islamic country for fundamentalism and jihad and though it attracts less attention than Iran its influence is probably greater. Pakistan owes the greater part of its prestige within Islam to Abu'l

A'la Maududi (1903–1979), whom many Muslims regard as the founder of modern fundamentalism.

Maududi's understanding of Islam was as a worldwide revolutionary movement led by true Muslims. Unlike many of his Arab associates, he was not a nationalist but an Islamist. 'Islam demands the earth,' he said, 'and will not settle for a part or section of it.' On this basis he had rejected the partition of India in 1947; for Maududi the whole of the sub-continent was Muslim, not just the area of Pakistan-to-be.

He constantly claimed the *Koran* as his authority for his type of jihad. 'The *Koran* does not contain mere opinions and abstract thoughts,' he wrote. '. . . It is not a book of discussing theology . . . it is a book of agitation and movement . . .'

As leader of the Jamaat-i-Islami (community of Islam) he was remarkably successful in Pakistan. His Jamaat movement was permitted to operate openly and was never banned when its activists committed violent acts against the law. Even when Maududi and other Jamaat leaders criticized the Pakistan government as 'un-Islamic' they were not punished. The shrewd Maududi knew that Pakistan, which had been created in the name of Islam, could not be seen to suppress the Jamaat.

The best organized political party in Pakistan, the Jamaat is generously funded by Saudi Arabia, with contributions also from Libya and Iran. It has a grand centre outside Lahore from where its activities reach into every corner of Pakistani life. A former journalist, Maududi knew the importance of the press and the Jamaat bought or founded hundreds of papers. In the name of jihad its activists are always ready to use violence to coerce opponents. The Jamaat's student body, Islami Jamiat-i-Talaba, is tremendously powerful and gives jihad its momentum. Since the early 1970s it has regularly won power in college elections and its organizers can provide tens of thousands of street demonstrators at very short notice.

Maududi's Jamaat, now led by Mian Tufail Muhammad, is an open supporter of General Zia al-Huq's military dictatorship. It colluded in the hanging of ex-Prime Minister Bhutto in 1979. It backs Zia's policy of 'Islamization from above' and his firm application of the laws of the Shari'a – floggings, amputations and stoning to death or beheading in the Saudi tradition.

Within Pakistan, jihad has been mainly directed against the biggest religious minority, the Ahmadiyya of Qadiana sect. Fanatical mullahs and fundamentalists kept up such a campaign of hate against the Ahmadiyyans, accusing them of being heretics, that in May 1984 the government decreed that they could neither call themselves Muslims nor use Muslim terms to describe their religious practices. Gradually Ahmadiyyans in state service are being removed from their posts; the Jamaat seems to have been influenced in this by the Iranians' persecution of its Bahi'a citizens. Christians and other minority groups, all of them targets for jihad, fear for their own future and that of Pakistan.

The Indian government also fears the march of jihad. India is the home of millions of Muslims who are often referred to, in the Pakistani press, as 'prisoners of the Hindus.' Pakistan has declared as jihad each of its wars against India and India fears the Pakistani development of 'the Islamic bomb.' Pakistan is the custodian of the Islamic nuclear bomb – though it has yet to produce a bomb. A secret plant near Islamabad produced enriched uranium for the first time during the early 1980s, thus bringing the bomb closer. Supposedly the enriched uranium is for research purposes but for nearly 10 years Pakistan permitted Colonel Gaddafi to finance the development of its nuclear industry and Gaddafi certainly did not have peaceful research in mind. Exasperated by Gaddafi's air of proprietorship in Pakistan's nuclear programme, General Zia cut that particular link with Gaddafi. Money for the programme now comes from several Islamic countries, including Iran.

A Pakistani metallurgist, Dr Abdel Qader Khan, who was trained in Holland, is in charge of the uranium enrichment programme at Khan Research Laboratories which employ a staff of 3,000 and which is protected by French-made surface-to-air missiles. During 1985 Zia told a British reporter, 'There are only five countries in the world which have the expertise for the enrichment of uranium. We are the sixth.'

TURKEY

Turkey is the only Islamic country to have broken away from the stranglehold of the theologians and turned itself into a modern secular state. Kemal Ataturk, president of Turkey from 1922 until 1938, blamed the Islamic religion for Turkey's backwardness. He replaced Islamic legal codes with Western models, he secularized education and ordered that the Arab alphabet was to be superseded by Latin characters. He barred wearing of the fez because it was a traditional symbol of the wearer's attachment to Islam and because he considered it ridiculous and demeaning.

Between 1960 and 1979 Turkey was beset by numerous economic and social problems. In the former year the army threw out the government and executed Prime Minister Menderes and some of his cabinet. Between 1961 and 1980 there were 19 governments, most of them flimsy coalitions.

In 1971 the military again removed a prime minister, Suleiman Demerel, and restored full civilian government in 1973. During the 1970s terrorism became endemic, with right-wing, left-wing and Islamic extremists all murdering indiscriminately. In December 1978 fierce fighting broke out in the town of Kahramanmaras and 150 people were killed. The violence was aimed at Shi'a Turks, possibly because Sunni Muslims, worried about the collapse of the Shah's regime in Iran, feared a threat from other Shi'a extremists.

In 1980 General Evren and a party of high-ranking officers dissolved parliament, banned all political parties and ruled by decree until Turgut Ozal of the Motherland Party was elected in democratic elections in 1983. Turkey's Western and democratic leanings make it vulnerable to Islamic fundamentalism because it can engage in anti-State activities which would be firmly suppressed in non-democratic countries. The upsurge in fundamentalism, combined with a campaign supported by some of its neighbouring Islamic countries for the Islamization of the country, worries liberal leaders, politicians and intellectuals.

President Evren, in a widely televised tour of conservative provinces in 1985, warned against attempts to restore theocracy in Turkey, 'a danger as serious as fascism or communism'. He appealed particularly to the conservative masses in rural areas to distinguish between 'normal' religious practices and fanaticism. The president was as aware as the public that the ayatollahs in next-door Iran had declared jihad against 'Turkish apostasy' in 1982. The aim of this jihad is to bring Turkey back into Islam. This would be 'a return to the eighth century,' Evren said.

The Islamic Jihad organization has a particular strategic interest in Turkey as the eastern gateway to Europe. In addition, after Egypt it is the second most populous country of the Middle East and it has one of the world's largest armed forces. The senior ayatollahs consider that such an important country, as a secular and not a theocratic state, is an affront to Islam.

Iranian agitators have stirred Turkish fundamentalists into various expressions of disagreement with the nation's rulers. For instance, the headman of a village near Denizli in western Turkey banned the watching of television in coffee shops during the time of prayer. He ordered a $50 fine for those who disobeyed his order to be in the mosque rather than in coffee shops during prayer times.

Preaching in an Istanbul district, a Muslim mullah ordered women to stop reading newspapers and watching television because they showed photographs of women 'dressed improperly or undressed.' In Izmir speakers at a rally of the newly established Welfare Party, a pro-Islamic group, pledged to set up a new order in Turkey where 'not even the fingernails of women would be seen in public.'

The Minister of Education, Vehbi Dincerler, ordered that all girls taking part in sports shows and parades on the occasion of Youth Day must wear baggy trousers covering their legs. For many years the girls had worn swimsuits or short tunics when they performed their gymnastic shows on that national holiday. This was the first time that such a measure was introduced and many Turks criticized it as a backward step.

All these incidents were relatively petty. Much more seriously, after a heated parliamentary debate, a decision was taken to build a mosque on the premises of the Turkish parliament. An opposition leader, Cahit Karakas, expressed the strong disapproval of many MPs. 'Parliament is a symbol of the modern republic,' he said, 'and of its principle of secularism. A mosque in this place is a denial of that principle.'

To stifle opposition to the mosque the chairman

of the judiciary committee introduced a bill providing for heavier penalties for 'insulting remarks against Allah and the Prophet Muhammad.' It has since been found that funds for building the mosque came from Saudi Arabia and that Saudi government ministers quietly told their Turkish counterparts that stronger trade ties would follow the building of the mosque.

For conservative or fundamentalist Turks the parliamentary mosque, the covering up of the female form, the dress of schoolgirls and punishment for 'offences against Allah' are collectively a normal manifestation of the nation's spiritual tendencies. For those Turks who favour liberal Westernization they are grave signs of a reactionary campaign designed to destroy the secular and modern structure of the nation.

The Minister of the Interior, Yildirim Akbulut, said late in 1985 that secret extremist organizations linked to foreign countries were conducting activities designed to provoke an Islamic revolution. Security departments around the country watch cases of Islamic fundamentalism very closely. They report that books, leaflets and other literature advocating an Islamic revolution and an end to secularism have been distributed in many areas. An independent member of parliament, Rustu Sardag, openly accused Iran and the Khomeini regime of systematically waging a propaganda campaign against Turkey's secular system.

The Motherland Party of the Prime Minister relies to a great extent on grass-roots, pro-religious conservative support. He sometimes warns Turks against criticizing Islamic countries and their leaders. Pragmatically, Ozal would like to placate the fundamentalists. His opponents see this as a sign of 'creeping Islam,' an insidious step-by-step approach advocated by some specialists in jihad.

Turkish newspapers throughout 1984–1987 warned that the behaviour of ruling party functionaries and in particular of some of the government ministers is starting to cause deep concern in progressive circles. The leading daily newspaper, *Milliyet*, published in an editorial: 'What some of these politicians are doing is contrary to the expectations of the people who are attached to Ataturk's reforms and particularly to the principle of secularism. These circles are dismayed by the ultra-conservative moves of the Motherland Party. This Party's politicians should understand that the preservation of these principles is as important as the efforts to improve the economy.'

The difficulty for the liberals and moderates is that the leaders of Islamic Jihad as well as the fundamentalist Saudi Arabian government and the imperialist Gaddafi have all made it clear to the Turkish leaders that by re-embracing Islam in the fight against the West they can gain a great deal of money for Turkey – money from oil. At present the United States subsidizes Turkey, which also gains a great deal from NATO countries. Should these benefits weaken, the advocates of holy war would quickly make inroads into Turkey.

It would be ironic indeed if military jihad swept

across Turkey because in 1915 Turkey, in the name of Islam, massacred 1.5 million Armenian Christian Turks living in Anatolia and brutally drove out most of those who survived. Turkey was then the homeland of the Ottoman Empire. The Kurds, an Islamic people, occupied the lands from which the Armenians were expelled. The Turkish leaders who instigated the massacre considered the near-extermination of the Armenian Christians as a major victory for holy war.

Kurdish nationalism, with its demand for a Kurdish homeland, is now steadily rising into prominence and, a further irony, the Muslim Kurds are aligning with Christian Armenian terrorist groups who, generations after the massacres, still exact revenge by killing Turkish diplomats and airline officials. Simultaneously the steady erosion of any vestiges of the historical presence of Armenians in eastern Turkey goes on. The last remaining churches, which are alien and embarrassing to the Muslim population of the area, are unlikely to be restored. The conflict seems endless. When Armenians killed a Turkish diplomat in Athens in the summer of 1980 they left a message saying, 'You declared holy war in 1915. You will still have it in 2015.'

SOVIET UNION

While Islamic Jihad and other Islamic fundamentalists consider that the Arab world, parts of the Islamic world and the West are major targets of holy war the Soviet Union has not been neglected.

Many Muslims outside the Soviet Union believe that in time Allah will destroy the Communist empire as they believe He destroyed the Christian crusaders and they are aiding the process.

In the 1960s the Soviet government began a campaign to 'liberate from religion' the 60 million people of its five Muslim states – Uzbekistan, Tadzhikistan, Turkmenia, Kirghizia and Kazakhstan. Only 30 Muslims a year are permitted to make the pilgrimage to Mecca as 'representatives of Soviet Islam.' Only a strictly limited number of copies of the *Koran* is available and there is only one *Koranic* school – in Uzbekistan.

Islamic radio programmes from Saudi Arabia, Iran and Pakistan are broadcast into the Soviet Central Asian republics where now more than 60 million Muslims live. Pakistani imams and writers in particular consider that a 'great striving' – the essence of holy war – is necessary to bring the Soviet Muslims back to a full Islamic life. Similarly some Iranians are working on long-term plans to turn the Soviet's Islamic states into one or more independent Islamic nations. Despite strict Soviet border control, mullahs sent by Islamic Jihad have penetrated into the southern republics where they distribute cassettes from Ayatollah Khomeini and copies of the *Koran*.

The Soviet government is well aware that 'tenacious religious prejudices' – a description of Muslim activity in an official report – are causing problems. They link the religious prejudices to the poor quality of Russian language teaching.

During 1985–86 the central government purged the regional governments of Turkmenia, Uzbekistan and Kazakhstan. Officials were sent from Moscow to take over from local Muslim leaders. Behind the removal of the Asian leaders is the determination of the Gorbachev regime to prevent the vast region from slipping into 'separateness.' The renewed stress on proper study of the Russian language springs from this but also from the need to prepare young Central Asian men for service in the Soviet army; one in 10 conscripts could be Uzbek by 1990. Yet the Uzbeks are still so profoundly Islamic that they believe that one day the great eleventh-century conqueror Tamurlane will return to lead them against the infidel Russians. His body in its black onyx tomb in Samarkand has a powerful influence on all Russian Muslims.

Just how the Communists will cope with revolutionary militant Islam and its holy war is one of the most fascinating questions of modern times for despite all the official endeavour to undercut Islam there were many signs in 1988 that Islamic consciousness was growing. For instance, two official mosques in the Tadzhik region of Kurgan-Tyube, bordering on Afghanistan, more than doubled their income from the performance of religious rites over the period 1982–1986. The number of Islamic 'holy places' has grown in Turkmenia. The Communist Party paper, *Pravda*, described how 'out-of-work people and criminals find an abandoned grave and declare that some holy figure was buried there. They go into the villages, persuade people to pray for the soul of the deceased and then begins a pilgrimage of the aged and of mainly illiterate people.'

An increase in the number of unofficial mullahs and the interest in Islam shown by young people also worry the central government. Official and unofficial reports show that the Muslim family and the wider clan around it resist official modernizing influences in favour of Islamic practices. That which most alarms Kremlin leaders is the high birth-rate; demographers predict 100 million Soviet Muslims by the end of the century. Official-dom has been unable to eradicate the practice of the sale of brides. In Uzbekistan a virgin costs 500 roubles, 200 kilos of flour, 50 kilos of rice, two sheets and nine suits.

CHAPTER THIRTEEN

Communiqués from the war fronts: Western Europe

Western Europe as a whole is caught up in jihad for two reasons.

Firstly, it is the major arena for assassination and terrorism directed against Muslim dissident escapees who have found refuge there.

Secondly, it is the target for holy war because Islamic fundamentalists oppose Christian beliefs and practices and because, in common with the entire Western world, it is 'decadent and evil.'

The first type of jihad is the more insidious and relentless. Poeple who have fled from Iran, Libya, Lebanon, Sudan, Syria and other Muslim countries may have found sanctuary in Western Europe, the United States or Canada but sanctuary is not necessarily safety. They are hunted by Islamic Jihad, Islamic Amal, Iranian terrorist groups, Colonel Gaddafi's death squads, Syrian death squads, the master terrorist Abu Nidal and various factions of the PLO. Virtually all these expatriates are, to their own governments, traitors and criminals. Those who have reached North America have found a safer life than those in Western Europe but not one is really safe from the vengeance of jihad.

Islam's jihad against the West itself – quite apart from Muslims *in* the west – is direct and unequivocal. One of the earliest expressions of modern jihad against the West was by the Pakistani author, Abul Hasan Ali Nadwi, in a pamphlet called *The New Menace and its Answer*, written for the Academy of Islamic Research based in Lucknow, India. Published several years before Khomeini's revolution in Iran, the Nadwi pamphlet has been the basis for several other pamphlets which seek to show the confrontation between Islam and the West as a 'battle.'

The battle that is being fought today is between Western materialism and Islam, the last of the messages of God. On one side is agnosticism and on the other the Divine Law (the Koran). I believe that this is the last struggle between religion and irreligiousness after which the world will swing full-scale towards one side or the other. The Jihad of today, the greatest need of the present hour, is to repulse this storm of atheism [that is, the Christian West] nay, to go ahead and make a direct assault at the heart of it . . . there is not a day to be wasted . . .

Dr S. M. Darsh, Imam of the London Central Mosques expressed more precise complaints in 1980. 'In the sphere of theology there is no giving up the battle . . . Christians are accused of misunderstanding the true nature of Jesus as a human being, accepting the pagan conception of a human god, defamation of the Supreme Being in ascribing incarnation to Him, accepting unfounded myths about the crucifixion and seeking to justify it in a way which denigrates human nature.'[1]

[1] *Muslims in Europe*, published by Ta-Ha Publishers, London.

Until the 1980s the most powerful Islamic weapon against the West was supposed to be the threat of oil sanctions; that is, the West's oil supply from the Persian Gulf would be cut off or sharply reduced. This would force the West to come to terms over various political and military issues, notably Western support for the right of Israel to exist. The 'oil weapon' had been used in 1973 and had caused panic in much of the West.

However, rapid and radical changes occurred. The oil states needed ever greater and greater income to finance their massive development programmes and this finance could come only from oil exports. Simultaneously the British, Dutch and Norwegians were developing their highly productive North Sea oilfields, thus lessening Western dependence on Middle East oil. The United States built up a tremendous oil 'strategic reserve' by filling caverns and tunnels with oil; thus US vulnerability to a Middle East oil boycott decreased. Throughout the world, during the 1980s, an oil glut built up so that prices fell. In their anxiety to maintain their high incomes, various States belonging to the Organization of Petroleum Exporting Countries (OPEC) undercut one another. The dominance of oil as a source of power was reduced by the alternative sources, such as nuclear and water power. The 'oil weapon' ceased to exist by 1980 though many leaders of Islamic Jihad as well as some rulers of oil states did not fully realize this fact until 1982.

The Western European countries against which

jihad has been most evident are Britain, France
(see earlier chapters), Italy and Spain.

During 1982–83 a holy war terror network
capable of launching suicide attacks against Western targets was formed, with recruiting centres in
London, Rome and Vienna. The ensan entehari
('suicide men') were from several Muslim countries, including Pakistan, Tunisia and Turkey. They
attended special Islamic courses before being sent
on to training courses in Iran.

BRITAIN

On 28 November 1984 the deputy British high
commissioner in Bombay, Mr Percy Norris, was
being driven to his office in a white Rover, a well-
known vehicle in the city. Neither Norris nor his
driver took any notice of two men carrying plastic
bags as the Rover slowed down on the approach to
a roundabout. They were Muslim assassins. As the
car slowed down they struck, firing three bullets.
Hit in the head and chest, Mr Norris did not live
long.

A spokesman for the Revolutionary Organization
of Socialist Muslims, calling a London news agency
from Bucharest, announced that Mr Norris had
been killed because 'Britain had ignored a warning
to stop the detention and torture of fighters . . . a
group of fighters of our organization carried out the
sentence of death.'

The organization's name was yet another cover
for the Abu Nidal or Black June terrorist group. In
March 1983 three of its members were gaoled for a

total of 95 years for the attempted assassination in London of Mr Shlomo Argov, the Israeli ambassador to Britain.

The same group had killed Mr Kenneth Whitty, First Secretary at the British Embassy in Athens, three months earlier. The day before Queen Elizabeth's tour of Jordan in March it had planted three bombs in Amman.

Writing in 1985, Anthony Hyman, a leading student of Muslim fundamentalism, noted[2] that in Western Europe (and North America) there were some 'striking recent initiatives of a fundamentalist or Pan-Islamic inspiration, nearly always relying on funds from one or more Muslim state.' He cited the Muslim Institute of London as a centre of Islamic research, 'aiming at making a positive presentation of Islam in the West' but concerned basically with Muslims living in the West and the young generation born there, which the Islamic leaders see as in 'danger' of assimilation into the local community.

According to Hyman, the Muslim Institute is linked to *The Crescent International* based in Toronto. This journal started in 1980 as 'news magazine of the Islamic movement.' Both the London institute and the Canadian journal, Hyman says, have a 'shrill strongly anti-Western bias and are enthusiastic supporters of the Iranian revolution.' The director of the Muslim Institute, Kalam

---

[2] In his booklet *Muslim Fundamentalism*, published by the Institute for the Study of Conflict, London.

Siddique, claims in one of many booklets that 'Western civilization is in fact a plague and a pestilence. It is no civilization at all. It is a disease . . .'

In 1981 a group of wealthy Saudi businessmen founded in London a monthly journal, *Arabia: The Islamic World Review*. This English-language journal declared that its aims were to provide 'more accurate information and more informed and perceptive comment from predominantly Muslim perspectives and to provide a forum for dialogue between Muslims and others on a whole range of issues . . .' Originally *Arabia* was interesting and independent but its policy was apparently criticized from within the Islamic world as in 1983 the editor complained that 'in every Muslim country there is a heightened tendency to believe in conspiracy theories and to ascribe ulterior motives to those questioning state policies and social practices.' The editor criticized a trend in the Muslim world which he described as 'political and intellectual introversion.' By 1985 *Arabia* itself seemed to be strongly under the influence of the fundamentalist tendency it had earlier criticized.

From time to time jihad commanders visit Britain. One of the most prominent was Ayatollah Ruhollah Khoiniha, Iran's chief prosecutor and outranked only by Ayatollahs Khomeini and Montazeri. In November 1983 Khoiniha arrived in London, travelling under an assumed name with a Syrian passport. He was supposed to organize Muslim students and workers and to open secret accounts in offshore banks in Jersey, Channel Islands. When he was discovered by the British Anti-Terrorist Squad, Khoiniha fled. Within five months of his visit up to 150 Revolutionary Guards and mercenaries had been sent to London to carry out attacks on Iranian opponents of the Khomeini régime.

According to a *Sunday Times* journalist, Amir Taheri, recruitment in Britain in 1983 and early 1984 was in the hands of Ayatollah Azri Qomi, a former prosecutor-general of revolutionary Iran (*Sunday Times* 8.1.1984).

The major jihad threat to Britain is from Gaddafi's holy war. In 1973 the Irish navy intercepted the motor vessel *Claudia*. On board was Joe Cahill, the former Belfast IRA leader, and large amounts of Libyan weapons and explosives, including 250 submachine guns, all intended for the IRA. Gaddafi later switched his allegiance to Protestant extremists, believing that they were more revolutionary.

In September 1985 it was clear that Libya was determined to supply weapons and explosives to terrorist groups in Britain and Ireland. This was a form of retaliation for the expulsion of Libyan diplomats from London and the British decision to break diplomatic relations following the shooting of WPC Yvonne Fletcher in St James Square. During a peaceful demonstration by opponents of Gaddafi, Miss Fletcher had been hit by a bullet fired from the 'Libyan People's Bureau' or quasi embassy.

Gaddafi's decision to again supply the IRA coincided with a decision by Irish republican organizations to seek arms from Libya. They already knew that Gaddafi was supplying grenades to a Palestinian group in London. Beginning in September 1985 British and Irish police began an intense and continuous surveillance operation on suspects with Libyan connections in an attempt to prevent arms and money from reaching the Provisional IRA and the Irish National Liberation Army.

While a few British people living abroad are selected as individual assassination targets, a greater number become chance victims of a wider form of holy war. In September 1985 a holy war terrorist in Athens threw grenades over the wall of a hotel garden and seriously wounded British tourists. The following month another Arab terrorist threw a bomb into the British Airways office in Rome, injuring 15 people, four of them seriously.

SPAIN

Spain is of key jihad strategic importance, as I have explained elsewhere, because of the perceived neeed for Islam to regain the great power and prestige it held in Spain for eight centuries.

Islamic Jihad's major attack against Spain occurred in Madrid in April 1985 when its agents exploded a bomb in a restaurant; 18 people were killed and 82 injured. A telephone call to Reuters news agency in Beirut warned that this was 'merely the first act' in the campaign. The attack was also directed against the United States; American military personnel at an air force base outside Madrid use the restaurant. Fifty Americans were among the 200 diners at the time of the explosion. The Spanish government also came under attack from Islamic Jihad for signing a treaty of friendship with Israel in 1986.

ITALY

The extent of Islamic Jihad's operations in Italy became known late in 1984 when the Italian police arrested a group of seven Shi'a Muslims accused of plotting to blow up the American embassy in Rome. The men came from the same group which made three major attacks against American installations in Beirut.

Following a tip-off from the Italian secret service, the Rome anti-terrorist squad had been watching the seven Lebanese for almost a year. Then the Swiss police arrested Hani Hussain Atat, a 21-year-old Lebanese Shi'a, at Zürich airport on 18 November. He was wearing a body belt stuffed with explosives. Atat and a colleague were couriers working over a long period on the transport of small quantities of explosives into Italy. Following the arrest of Atat, the Italian police picked up the rest of the gang.

Investigators found pictures of Ayatollah Khomeini in one of the flats they raided, with propaganda material and leaflets referring to jihad. Some evidence of the amount of money paid to holy war fighters working abroad came out of this investigation. Each of the seven men in Rome received £2,000 a month.

Italian police reported to their government in 1986 that the Iranian ambassador to the Holy See – the Vatican – was directing a network of holy war operations in Spain, Italy, West Germany, Britain and France. The ambassador concerned was Ayatollah Khosrow-Shahi, who is believed by Western intelligence sources to have arranged the killing of a former Iranian anti-Khomeini general and the United Arab Emirates ambassador to France. The Italian police dossier on Khosrow-Shahi includes photographs of him making payments to various individuals for what is termed 'exportation of the Islamic revolution.'

The main recruiting office for young Shi'a volunteers was, in 1986, at 361–63 Via Nomentana, Rome. This is next door to the Libyan Embassy at 365 Via Nomentana. The two compounds are known to have tunnel connection. Khosrow-Shahi was once Khomeini's chauffeur and bodyguard and in 1979 was believed to be second in command of the group which organized the seizure of the US Embassy in Teheran.

FRANCE

On 4 September 1981 the French ambassador in Lebanon, Louis Delamare, was seriously wounded when a gunman walked up to his car which had stopped at a Beirut roadblock and fired several 7.65mm bullets into him. The ambassador's driver, who was unhurt, drove to the nearest hospital but Delamare died an hour later. Beirut political circles were distressed for Delamare had many friends,

but they were not really surprised. They knew that
the French would become targets.

A rumour quickly spread that Syria was behind
the assassination. Damascus had no lack of reasons
for hitting at France and expressing in this manner
its objections to the initiative France was taking in
the Middle East, notably in favour of a settlement
of the crisis in Lebanon which Syria considered its
own backyard. France was accused specifically of
promoting the idea of a rebuilt Lebanese army
capable of taking over from the so-called Arab
Deterrent Force, really a Syrian force, which was
supposed to have been guaranteeing law and order
in a large part of Lebanon since 1975.

The French security forces date the holy war
against them from the day of Delamare's murder.
The Iranians, as Syria's ally, were directly involved
from the beginning. They objected to France's
arms sales to Iraq and to the political asylum
offered to the former Iranian president Abolhassan
Bani-Sadr. Together the Syrian and Iranian leaders
objected to a recent visit to Israel by the French
president, to the cordial reception given in Paris to
some of the Syrian government's opponents and to
official French criticism of the Syrian-Iranian alliance as 'unholy.'

French investigators found that Delamare had
been killed by a hit squad only very recently
formed – a branch of the Syrian secret service
known as the Red Knights. It is a para-military
body, operating from Beirut, and dedicated to holy
war. Its nominal head was then Rifaat Assad, the

Syrian president's brother, and its membership was remarkably diverse. Its recruits came from terrorists of the pro-Syrian Saiqa organization, Lebanese involved in clan and political party feuds, Shi'as from the Amal group, Palestinians who had broken with the Popular Front for the Liberation of Palestine and with Fatah. The Red Knights took some kind of Islamic oath and were then trained at one of Syria's best protected camps between Tartus and Latakia; the principal instructors were Bulgarian.

Despite the assassination of its ambassador the French government did not change its Middle East policy. Holy war then moved to France. On 19 December 1981 a parcel bomb was found at a government office and was defused just 18 minutes before it was timed to explode. The material used to make the bomb was traced to a cultural attaché at the Syrian embassy. On 30 March 1982 a bomb exploded on the Paris–Toulouse express. This incident again attracted suspicion to the Syrian embassy and to another cultural attaché, Mikhail Kassouha – who was in fact a member of the Syrian secret service. He was suspected of having tried to set up a Red Knights recruiting office in Paris.

In the period 1980–1986 more terrorist attacks took place in France than in any other country, with a total of 162 bombings. In 1984 *The Times* called Paris 'the most lethal terrorist capital of Europe.' Not all the bombings and other attacks were the work of Islamic Jihad and its affiliated groups. French security chiefs cannot apportion precise blame for terrorist incidents because various terror groups are affiliated; for instance, Islamic Jihad and the main French terrorist organization Action Directe have close ties for their mutual benefit.

Islamic Jihad shocked the French people on 8 March 1986 when its gunmen kidnapped a four-man French television crew in Beirut. The crew, from Antennae 2, went to the city after claims that Michel Seurat, one of four Frenchmen kidnapped earlier, had been executed in reprisal for France's deportation of two pro-Iranian Iraqis to Baghdad. These two, Fawzi Hamzeh and Hassan Kheireddine, had been arrested in a police anti-terrorist drive in February, after a series of bombings in Paris. In Baghdad they were seen as traitors who had gone over to the Iranians.

In entering the strongly Shi'a district of Jnah to photograph a meeting of Hezbollah members, the French TV men showed profound ignorance of Shi'a hatred for France or a courageous professional indifference to danger – or both. They actually filmed the Hezbollah meeting, a further indiscretion.

The French President and Prime Minister both responded with declarations that France would not free Iranian and Lebanese Shi'a terrorists and said that they were in no position to demand that Iraq free the two pro-Iranian activists returned to Baghdad. The Prime Minister said, 'To yield to blackmail, which is also being exercised against other great nations, would put French people in danger all over the world. They would run the risk of being taken as hostages by groups exploiting the anguish of their families so that their fanaticism can triumph.'

Nevertheless, in 1987, the French government did yield to blackmail. This followed a rupture in Franco-Iranian relations in mid-1987. French police wished to question Wahid Gordji, 34, an interpreter at the Iranian embassy in Paris, in connection with terrorist bombings in Paris that killed 11 people and injured 161 in September 1986. Gordji was said to be a ringleader of a Europe-wide Iranian intelligence network linked to holy war terrorism.

In response, the Iranians claimed that enemies of the Khomeini régime had been helped by French diplomats in Teheran and kept the diplomats as prisoners in their embassy. The complex impasse led to deals between Iran and France. France expelled some leading anti-Khomeini fugitives and paid to have some hostages freed in Lebanon – though the government denied that ransom money was paid. In similar deals, the West German government paid ransoms to have German hostages released.

The French had a significant victory against Gaddafi's holy war. In September 1987 they stopped a ship named the *Eksun* on suspicion of smuggling narcotics, only to find a large cargo of arms and explosives. They were en route from Libya to Ireland for the IRA.

In January 1988 the Muslim Institute of Britain organized, in London, the 'Haramine Conference' which was attended by delegates of extreme Islamic groups from 40 Muslim countries. The majority of those attending were Sunni Muslims, yet they voted to accept Ayatollah Khomeini as the true spititual leader and 'the authentic voice of Islam' for both Sunni and Shi'a Muslims.

CHAPTER FOURTEEN

Other battle fronts, other victims

Jihad requires persistent continuity and recognizes no moderation. This is one of the principles taught by the senior instructors of holy war, men such as Sheikh Tufaile and Hussein Rezaie, who teach terror tactics at the Hotel Khawam in Baalbek, taken over by Islamic Jihad and turned into a training school. From a dilapidated building in downtown Baalbek known as 'Hosseineh', which serves as the Bekaa Valley headquarters for the Revolutionary Guards, Tufaile, Rezaie and others – including liaison officers from the Syrian half of the PLO – plan some holy war operations. Others are planned from Damascus and Teheran. They include assassination of individuals, intimidation and oppression of entire non-Muslim minority communities; hijacking of aircraft; kidnappings to obtain hostages; infiltration of nations with large Muslim minorities; incitement of fundamentalists to rebel against Muslim governments which are not considered sufficiently Islamic.

This is a selection of such holy war operations.

Iran's Anglicans
Hardly had the Ayatollah Khomeini taken over Iran in February 1979 when Aristo Sayeh, the Anglican vicar in Shiraz, was found with his throat cut. A

notice was scrawled on the wall with his blood. *Jihad will have its way*. That summer the Iranian mullahs seized an Anglican hospital and a school for the blind in Isfahan. Then they began to intimidate churchmen to force them to reveal a supposedly missing cache of money.

In October 1979 in Isfahan two gunmen burst into the bedroom of Anglican Bishop Hassan Barnaba Dehqani-Tafti and his British wife Margaret and sprayed them with automatic-pistol fire. Four bullets hit the pillow near the bishop's head and his wife was wounded in the arm. The bishop, who was president of the Central Synod, which includes all Anglicans in the Middle East, fled to exile in Cyprus. His British secretary, Jean Waddell, remained behind and on 1 May 1980 a death squad entered her apartment in search of another Anglican clergyman. First they began to strangle her, then they fired two shots into her head. She survived though a week later the bishop's son, Bahram, 24, was murdered with shots in the head and chest.

The Anglican Church had existed in Iran for 150 years and in 1980 had 1,000 followers, most of them Muslim converts. The attacks ordered by the ayatollahs were aimed at driving out the 'colonialist missionaries'. In addition, many of the Anglicans who refused to re-embrace Islam were murdered.

The Baha'is

The Baha'i people of Iran, followers of a non-political religion, were among the first groups against whom Ayatollah Khomeini declared holy war. He accused them of being 'spies for the American CIA, for the Soviet KGB or for world Zionism.'

His real reason for oppressing them is that they are not an Islamic sect although they live within Islam. Their founder was the Persian Siyyid Ali Muhammad, known as the Bab, who announced himself in 1844 as the herald of a saviour who would bring a new era of peace and light. Baha'ism prohibits participation in politics, condemns superstition and prejudice, practises total equality between men and women, insists on strict monogamy as well as chastity before marriage and fidelity afterwards. Baha'is are not missionaries and strictly observe the law of the land in which they live.

Even during the relatively enlightened reign of the Shah, Iran's mullahs and the army had tacit government approval to make life difficult for the Baha'is but they were not persecuted. Under the regime of Ayatollah Khomeini their religion is 'criminal' and all Baha'i activities are banned. The religion is hated by fundamentalist Muslims because it is based on the teachings of a prophet who came after Muhammad; hence it can have no validity, even though it honours Muhammad. As a peaceful, thriving, successful and educated community the Iranian Baha'is attracted animosity from the militant Muslims.

Between Khomeini's seizure of power in 1979 and the end of 1987 more than 250 Baha'is were executed and 76 disappeared and are presumed dead. In December 1987 700 were in prison and many had been tortured. As part of the holy war against them the Baha'is are constantly terrorized; they can own no property, they are not entitled to a job, their bank deposits have been seized and professional certificates withdrawn. Baha'i holy places, including cemeteries, have been desecrated or destroyed.

About 45,000 of Iran's 500,000 Baha'is had fled from Iran to the end of 1985; those who remained lived under a suspended sentence of death. Khomeini had issued the edict: 'If somebody is a heretic and will not recant, the shedding of his blood is not a crime.' The Baha'is would live in fear until Khomeini or his successor rescinded this edict which was, in effect, an invitation and incitement to fanatics to kill Baha'is.

The Yazidis

A confederation of tribes with a religion based on Zoroastrianism, the one million Yazidis live in adjoining parts of Iran and Iraq. They regarded the Iran-Iraq war as 'Islamic fanaticism', from which they themselves have suffered in the past. When they refused to fight in the warring armies those in Iran became victims of declared jihad while those in Iraq became subject to tacit but undeclared jihad.

In 1982 the Yazidis' supreme chief, Prince Muawwiah Esmaeel Yazidi, travelled to France to publicize his peoples' case. Press-gangs were being sent into the hills to seize tribesmen, young and old, for army service. Those who still refused to fight were either killed or imprisoned. In Iran, he said, black-lists of Yazidi villages and tribes had been prepared by local Shi'a vigilante groups so that genocide could begin when the Gulf War ended. 'Both Khomeini's ayatollahs and his supporters in Iraq are determined to finish us off,' the prince said. 'The Iranian ayatollahs consider us as enemies of Allah and because of this ruling they will spare nobody.'

The Yazidis do much that is abhorrent to Muslims; they drink wine, eat pork, marry only one wife and base their society on an ancient caste system with four basic groups – princes, priests, warriors and workers. To Shi'a Muslims in particular princes should never precede priests.

The Kuwait Airlines Hijack: December 1984

Events surrounding the hijack of an Airbus between Kuwait and Pakistan and taken to Teheran were an overt holy war action and declared as such by the Shi'a hijackers. The gang was seeking to force the release from Kuwaiti prisons of 17 Shi'as convicted of terrorist acts against American, French and Kuwaiti targets in Kuwait in December 1983.

Having forced the British pilot to fly to Teheran, the hijackers threatened and maltreated the passengers – most of whom were Sunni Kuwaitis and Pakistanis – and shot dead two Americans. Another American was beaten and burned with cigarette ends. The aircraft sat on the airport runway for six

days before the Iranians took any decisive step, a
circumstance which convinced the Kuwait government of Iranian collusion in the hijack. Iran's
strange behaviour certainly suggested a degree of
complicity. For one thing, the previous month the
Iranian security forces had acted within hours when
a Saudi airliner was hijacked to Teheran by Yemeni
hijackers.

The Economist's Levant correspondent, investi-
gating the episode, noted that explosives, wiring
and lengths of rope for tying up the hostages
appeared on board the aircraft. 'It would have been
difficult for the hijackers to bring all that equip-
ment with them,' he wrote. 'It is even more
peculiar that the Iranians widely publicized the
hijackers' actions, including their ill-treatment of
the passengers. And the eventual "rescue" had the
appearance of a put-up job.' It was easy to draw
this inference. Four hours after the hijackers had
made their wills and said their final prayers before
their intended blowing up of the aircraft they asked
for cleaners to tidy it up – and the 'cleaners'
overpowered them. Another clue to collusion was
that the Iranian authorities refused to permit a
Kuwaiti negotiating team which was sent to Teheran to have any contact either with the hijackers
or with the Kuwaiti co-pilot and a wounded Kuwaiti
security guard.

The words of a Kuwaiti passenger threatened
with death were relayed from the cockpit of the
aircraft to the control tower and made a deep
impression throughout the Arab world. He said:

'How can you kill me? I am a Muslim like you.'
This was followed by the sound of a shot, which
turned out to be a hoax. The Kuwaiti passengers
were beaten on the steps of the plane and then
dragged inside. Tomato sauce was poured over
them and the terrorists then demanded that a local
photographer be sent on board to take pictures of
the 'bodies.' The incident aroused Sunni Muslim
anger against the Shi'as and hardened the resolve
of the Kuwaiti leaders not to release their prisoners
from gaol. The Iranian authorities promised to put
the hijackers on public trial but if any action was
taken against them it was never disclosed. The
Kuwaiti authorities were convinced that the terrorists were allowed to go free on the grounds that
'holy war warriors cannot be punished for their
actions.'

The Buckley kidnapping: March 1984
William Buckley, aged 57, was the CIA station
chief at the American Embassy in Beirut, though
his cover title was 'political officer.' He spent much
of his time developing information that might prevent terrorist attacks on Americans in the Middle
East but was not involved in violence himself.
Kidnapped on 16 March 1984, he was taken to the
eastern Bekaa, where the Syrians disclosed his true
role in Lebanon to the Hezbollah terrorists. He
was tortured and interrogated over a long period.
In March 1985, disguised as a wounded soldier, he
was transported secretly by air from Damascus to
Teheran. In the basement of the Iranian foreign

ministry he was again tortured. Moved to a holy war training camp near the city of Qum he died of a heart attack induced by torture and captivity. Full details of Buckley's ordeal were disclosed by Jack Anderson of *The Washington Post*, quoting intelligence sources.

Other kidnappings

Islamic Jihad squads seized, at different times, US Associated Press correspondent Terry Coleman; a Roman Catholic priest, the Rev Lawrence Jenco; dean of the faculty of agriculture at the American university of Beirut, Thomas Sutherland; AUB's hospital administrator, David Jacobsen; an AUB librarian, Peter Kilburn; Presbyterian minister Benjamin Weir (released in September 1985); Alex Collett, a British official working for UNWRA; John McCarthy, a British journalist, Terry Waite, envoy of the Archbishop of Canterbury.

The Bucharest assassination: December 1984

Mr Asmi al Mufti, Counsellor at the Jordanian Embassy in Bucharest and the son of a former prime minister of his country, was killed as he walked out of his city hotel to take his five-year-old son to school. Mr Mufti and his family had previously been stationed in Beirut and were staying in the hotel until their apartment was ready. In Jordan he was a leader of the Circassian community, a group which traditionally provides King Hussein's bodyguards. The killing was claimed as an act of holy war.

The Jordanian airliner hijack: June 1985
Shi'a gunmen, having hijacked a plane belonging
to the Royal Jordanian Airlines, blew it up at Beirut
on 12 June. This was a direct action in the jihad
declared against King Hussein by the Shi'a Muslim
world aided and abetted by the Syrians. His immediate 'sin' was that he had backed Yasser Arafat's
PLO against that faction of the PLO controlled by
Syria and supported by the Shi'as.

The TWA Hijack: June–July 1985
The hijacking of a TWA passenger airliner was the
eighth aircraft hijacking by Lebanese and Iranian
Shi'a terrorists but it involved a new element: For
the first time a government minister – Nabih Berri,
the Minister of Justice in the Lebanese government
– was directly involved. The Lebanese government
thus not only failed to take action against the
hijackers aboard the aircraft but allowed them to
use Beirut as an operational headquarters. Berri
was personally in charge of these operations for
much of the time. Three other countries were
directly involved – Iran, Syria and Algeria. Planning began in Teheran in April when Ayatollah
Khomeini and two senior aides, probably Ayatollahs Khoiniha and Fazollah Mahalati, discussed
new terrorist operations and ways of carrying out
attacks against Western targets. Syria was implicated because it effectively controls Lebanon and
was able to give direct support to the hijackers.
The plane landed twice in Algeria but the Algerian
authorities made no attempt to detain the hijackers

or the aircraft. One of the American hostages was
murdered and his body thrown from the aircraft.
Passengers with 'Jewish-sounding names' were separated from the rest of the passengers, an alarming
development in holy war against the West. After a
terrifying 17-day ordeal the hostages were
released.

The Cairo murder: August 1985
A young Israeli cultural attaché was murdered by a
gunman connected with the Abu Nidal organization. Interviewed by the Arab newspaper *Al
Kaba*, Abu Nidal gave some 'background' to the
killing. 'Over there,' he said, 'is an organization of
educated young soldiers calling themselves revolutionary Egyptians. Their aim is holy war – to undo
Camp David and restore Egypt to its real place at
the centre of the Arab world. I fight with them.'

The Rome and Vienna massacres: December 1985
In simultaneous attacks on 27 December terrorists
of the Abu Nidal organization attacked passengers
waiting in airline check-in queues, killing 15 of
them and wounding 119. Privately, Gaddafi
claimed 'credit' for authorizing the massacres, and
publicly referred to them as 'heroic operations by
Palestinian martyrs.' The Iranian administration
labelled the massacres 'honourable actions in holy
war.'

Yugoslavia
In August 1983 Yugoslavian courts sentenced 18
Bosnian Muslims to long prison terms for 'political

and religious activism.' The case received no publicity in the West because the government did not
wish it to be known that Yugoslavia was a target for
jihad. The growth of Islam is most notable in Bosnia
which became Muslim under Turkish rule in the
16th century. Several hundred new mosques have
been built in recent years, many with financial help
from Islamic countries. *Borba*, the semi-official
daily newspaper published in Belgrade, complains
of 'increasing militancy' among Yugoslavia's Muslims, who make up 16 per cent of the population of
23.5 million. Despite these complaints, Yugoslavia
has become a base for Muslim terrorists, as a long
series of events indicate. The most significant link
was the flight of Abu Abbas, the militant PLO
leader who planned the *Achille Lauro* piracy in
October 1985. When the Italian authorities
released him he sought sanctuary in Yugoslavia,
where he was protected before returning to Syria.
Islamic Jihad's planners expect to be able to use
Yugoslavia as their base in Eastern Europe if only
because of the assured sympathy of the Bosnian
Muslims.

Indonesia

With a population of 160 million, Indonesia is the
biggest Islamic country in the world but its government is implacably opposed to the concept of a
Muslim state. However, the region of Aceh, in
northern Sumatra, is as fully an Islamic society as
Iran.

Having waged a true Islamic jihad against the

Dutch colonial government for 25 years earlier this
century, the Darul Islam movement of Aceh almost
broke away from Indonesia soon after its formation
as a republic. It agreed to stay only after it was
given local autonomy, complete with the supremacy of Islamic law, customs and social mores. Aceh
claims the title of Indonesia's 'verandah on Mecca'
both because it is the last port of call for Indonesian
pilgrims to Mecca and because the fierce orthodoxy
of the Acehese is supposed to be close to 'Mecca
Islam', that is, the pure Islam of the Prophet
Muhammad.

Since 1981 Iranian mullahs sent by the Khomeini
regime, as well as political agents from Gaddafi and
the Saudi government, have been inciting the
Acehese to be even more fundamentalist. The Iranians succeeded in inducing Daud Baruah, the leader
of the Darul Islam movement, to declare holy war
against President Suharto's regime. The government responded by placing Baruah under house
arrest in Jakarta.

The Acahese have been trying for years to force
out the large Chinese community in their midst;
there is a close parallel between the Chinese in
Aceh and the Baha'i people in Iran. Strong military
forces are stationed in or close to Aceh to contain
the violence which the government expects. It is
reluctant to take too forceful a line with the
Acehese who run a parallel administration that is
the effective government of Aceh, especially in
matters of law and order. Indonesia's president is
known to fear assassination at the hands of the

increasingly militant jihad warriors who are well supplied with weapons and explosives from abroad.

Against the Muslim Brotherhood

That the Muslim Brotherhood should become a *victim* of holy war might appear ironic because it has always believed in holy war and advocated it. The Brotherhood defines its creed this way: 'Allah is our aim, the Prophet Muhammad our only leader, the *Koran* our constitution, the holy war our way forward and death in that holy war our desire above all others.'

Founded by Hassan al-Banna in Egypt in 1928, the Brotherhood demanded 'absolute adherence to the objective of a totally Islamic state.' It has always preached that Western civilization created all the major ideological 'evils' – capitalism, fascism, communism. Much of the holy war's policy is consistent with that of the Iranian ayatollahs.

After its foundation – on a political, social, religious and economic base – the Brotherhood spread to a number of Muslim countries. It tried to assassinate President Nasser of Egypt in 1954 on the ground that he was not adequately Islamic. Six Brethren were then executed and many others were imprisoned. Later some members tried to murder President Sadat when they discovered that his 'revolution' was socialist rather than Islamic. 'The Egyptian government is damned because it denies the sovereignty of Allah,' one of the Brotherhood's publications proclaimed in 1978.

The Brotherhood's intention of imposing its own

militant and fundamentalist standards of Islamic behaviour on the whole Muslim community, by force if necessary, brought it into direct conflict with the Assad regime in Syria in the 1980s. The Assad faction is part of the Alawite community, which forms only 10 per cent of Syria's mainly Sunni Muslim population. The Brotherhood, with rigid beliefs in Islamic purity, does not accept the Alawites as Muslims.

Hama was the Syrian centre for Muslim Brotherhood members and their families and, according to the Syrian government, they proposed an uprising against the government. This seems unlikely because the Muslim Brotherhood has never been strong in numbers and prefers to incite unrest among the general public. On the justification of jihad against the Brotherhood the Syrian army was sent into Hama, in February 1982, to suppress the 'traitorous Brotherhood.' The army's actions in the city have become known as 'the massacre of Hama.' Amnesty International, from on-the-ground evidence, published a detailed report and put the number of dead at 20,000. The *Washington Post* expressed its statistics more graphically – 'as many as 20,000 orphans may have been created.' Other estimates are as high as 40,000 dead. Satellite photographs of Hama taken early in February contrast sharply with those taken later in the month. In the first set numerous mosques with their distinctive minarets can be seen; in the second set these minarets have disappeared. The mosques, apparently used by the Brotherhood as

bases, had been knocked down by shellfire or
tanks. During holy war, the regime later said, such
destruction was not sacrilege.

Amnesty reported that 6,000 to 8,000 Syrian
soldiers including units from the 21st Armoured
Division and the 47th Independent Armoured Brigade were sent to the city. However, another unit
was the Chemical Warfare Section; these soldiers
brought cyanide canisters, connected them to
rubber pipes at the entrances to buildings and
turned on the gas, killing all the inhabitants.
Amnesty claimed to have evidence of this action
and also reported that people were assembled at
the sports stadium and at military barracks and left
in the open for days without food or shelter, in
mid-winter. The entire operation took two weeks
because Hama is honeycombed with alleyways and
passages and the troops had orders to search every
room. Many innocent people must have been killed
because the Muslim Brotherhood had nothing like
20,000 members in Hama.

Two other élite corps had men in Hama at the
time of the slaughter. One was Brigades for the
Defence of the Revolution (Saraya al-Difa 'an al-
Thawra) which was led by the President's brother,
Rifaat Assad. The other was the Special Units (Al-
Wahdat al-Khassa) a commando-paratrooper corps
of 7,000 men commanded by Ali Haidar. The
Special Units tracked down the men who had
allegedly organized the uprisings; Rifaat Assad's
men interrogated them. The tortures used are
described in the Amnesty report (*Report from*

Amnesty International to the Government of the Syrian Arab Republic, December 1983, 65pp, £2).

Against the United States

Most of the millions of Muslims who live in the United States or who are there as students are *not* 'sleeping' holy war warriors waiting to be activated. But the American security authorities know that their Muslim communities have been infiltrated and that Iranian, Libyan and Lebanese Shi'a murder squads are at large. In such an enormous population in a large country it would be surprising if the FBI and other agencies could maintain surveillance on all possible threats to the nation's leaders.

The murder of Americans abroad and the attacks on American installations amply demonstrate that the US is regarded as a major enemy. In any case, Ayatollah Khomeini and President Gaddafi have declared it to be the 'Great Satan,' 'the Number One terrorist state,' and the 'Bloodsucker of the Third World.' Speeches by the hundred have been made against the US and its citizens and while oral holy war is rich in rhetoric there is no reason to doubt the seriousness of the threats. Those Americans who have witnessed the brutality of Muslim hijackers and pirates towards Americans selected as holy war victims have spoken of 'deliberate and sadistic cruelty.'

What happened to Robert Stethem, an American naval diver in his early twenties, was typical of the 'punishment' inflicted on representatives of the

'Great Satan.' Stethem was a passenger in June 1985 on TWA flight 847 from Athens to Rome, when it was seized by two terrorists from Lebanese Shi'a Amal. A 16-year-old Australian girl in the adjoining seat to Stethem later described what happened: 'They tried to knock him out with the butt of a pistol – and kept hitting him over the head, but he was very strong and they could not knock him out . . . They dumped him in his seat next to me and left him for ages. I tried to nurse him but there wasn't a great deal I could do. Later they dragged him away and shot him.' When finally the aircraft was brought down in Beirut Stethem's mutilated corpse was thrown out on to the tarmac.

In this hijack the terrorists articulated three of the consistent demands of Islamic Jihad and two other demands of a type frequently made in several parts of the world.

The primary demands were these:

- the United States must change its policies in the Middle East.
- President Mubarak of Egypt must be instantly overthrown.
- King Hussein of Jordan must be deposed or abdicate at once.

The secondary demands:

- Kuwait must release the 17 Shi'a terrorists being held in Kuwaiti prisons.

● Spain must release two imprisoned Shi'a terrorists.

No practical way existed in which the terrorists'
extravagant demands could possibly be met and to
that extent they were fantasies, but none the less
terrifying for the hostages caught up in what one of
the terrorists called 'this sacred adventure.'

Most hijack victims have been beaten up before
being shot. The staff of the American embassy in
Teheran, held as hostages for 444 days, were
subjected to psychological as well as physical cruelty. On numerous occasions the hostages were
lined up as for execution from the rear only to hear
a Kalashnikov trigger fall on an empty chamber.
For months on end they were forbidden to speak,
a form of torture calculated to break their spirit. At
least one hostage tried to commit suicide and two
suffered severe mental breakdowns.

The most ardent holy war warrior opposed to the
United States government and to certain of its
minority communities is himself American and
resident in the United States. He is Louis Farrakhan, who is highly regarded by Colonel Gaddafi as
'a gift of Allah' to the blacks of America. Formerly
Louis Eugene Walcott, Farrakhan was a Chicago
nightclub entertainer when he answered the call of
'The Honorable' Elijah Muhammad, who
announced himself as the Messenger of Allah.

Walcott changed his name to Louis X and became
second only to Malcolm X who preached that Allah
would soon consume the earth in a holy fire that
would fry only the 'white devils', permitting the

black 'original people' to rule the world. Malcolm X openly attacked his leader Elijah Muhammad and was shot dead in a Harlem ballroom by three Muslims; Farrakhan was allegedly implicated in the murder. Elijah Muhammad presented Farrakhan with a mosque in New York. By the 1970s members of the Muslim death squads from coast to coast were decapitating their victims and leaving the heads ritualistically facing the decadent West, away from holy Mecca.

Farrakhan broke away from the mainstream movement and set up the 'Nation of Islam.' Until the 1984 presidential campaign and the candidacy of the black Chicago preacher Jesse Jackson, Farrakhan remained a relative nobody. Jackson accepted his support and invited him to become part of the campaign. This gave Farrakhan his chance for national publicity.

Anti-semitic remarks and pro-Nazi praise became his stock in trade. Hitler was a 'great German' and 'a very great man.' Gaddafi saw in Farrakhan an articulate, vigorous representative and gave him a $5 million interest-free loan. The embarrassed Jesse Jackson broke away from Farrakhan who began to draw large crowds to hear his anti-white, anti-government, anti-Jewish speeches; 25,000 people crowded Madison Square Garden to hear him in 7 October 1985.

'The Jews are the skunks of the planet earth,' he told his audience. At another time he warned his enemies, 'If you rise up to kill me then Allah promises that he will bring on this generation the blood of the righteous . . . All of you will be killed outright.' He threatened the lives of the many black leaders who condemn him. The mayor of Los Angeles, George Deukmejian, has denounced Farrakhan and compared him to the Ku Klux Klan, American Nazis and other 'messengers of hate.'

Black editor-publisher Bill Tatum of New York's *The Amsterdam News*, wrote an angry editorial entitled 'Farrakhan's Final Solution.' He said that the US black leadership should shout down Farrakhan in defiance of his death threats against black leaders who oppose him.

The subject of Farrakhan has come up in meetings of representatives of the Iran-Syrian-Libyan alliance. Islamic Jihad regards Farrakhan as the principal publicist for holy war in the United States while Gaddafi believes that his 'Nation of Islam' can be used for overt attacks on American targets. The Syrians are more interested in using Farrakhan as a source of embarrassment to the American government. According to credible sources Farrakhan's bodyguards have been trained in Syria.

In January 1986 the British government refused to grant Farrakhan a visa to visit the United Kingdom; the Home Secretary decided that Britain had faced enough problems of security against holy war activists without importing more with Farrakhan.

CHAPTER FIFTEEN
The PLO and holy war

In Khartoum on 15 October 1985 PLO agents using the classic techniques of the *agent provocateur* – a whispering campaign, distributing of leaflets, promise of rewards – got together a crowd of 40,000 to listen to a speech by Yasser Arafat, chairman of the PLO. He had been permitted to visit Sudan only on the understanding that he would not arrange demonstrations. He kept to his word – the demonstrations were 'spontaneously' arranged by others.

The event is not significant but what Arafat told his audience is significant in the history of modern holy war.

The Arab revolution is alive in the Arab conscience in spite of imperialist and Zionist conspiracies. Reagan has decided to assassinate the PLO leadership in the belief that by so doing the revolution would come to an end. This is not so. The holy war and the armed struggle will escalate . . . I tell Reagan and his agents in our Arab world that the will of the Arab nation is from the will of Allah. Therefore, the Arab nations will be victorious.

Arafat based his attacking speech on the American action of seizing the *Achille Lauro* pirates while they were being flown from Egypt. By this reference to American agents in the Arab world he meant President Mubarak of Egypt, among others. The PLO agents led about 1,000 demonstrators in a riotous march to the US Embassy in Khartoum, where riot police using tear gas dispersed them.

Arafat's use of the holy war concept and reference to the 'will of Allah' was tacit admission of the Islamization of the PLO, a process which had been taking place for some years. It was not the first time Arafat had referred to jihad. He did so at the Islamic summit meeting in Lahore in 1974 and again at the Taif Summit in 1981. For some years he had been an active member of the Muslim Brotherhood so he was thoroughly indoctrinated with jihad directed against Arab governments. He fled from Egypt in 1957 because of danger of arrest as a Muslim Brotherhood subversive. He had openly declared himself mujihad – one who performs the duty of jihad.

However, in Khartoum his vehement support for jihad in his speech was much more than an individual oath of belief; as chairman of the PLO he was calling for holy war. In effect, he was announcing that the PLO was following the Shi'a attitude to war. Arafat is a Sunni Muslim, as are most members of the PLO. The organization also has Christian members; George Habash, leader of the Popular Front for the Liberation of Palestine (PFLP) is Greek Orthodox.

With its mixture of Marxist, Ba'thist and nationalist groups the PLO, right from its inception in 1964, was a model of the larger Arab world of which it was part; it had all the same rifts and

antagonisms. Arafat's own group, Fatah, was
simply nationalist. The PFLP was Marxist and
Habash's policy became ever more extreme; he
regarded himself as 'Marxist-Leninist' and he saw
the issue of Palestine not merely as part of an Arab
revolution but as essential to world revolution. The
arch-enemy was 'imperialism' of which 'the Zionist
enemy' was one spearhead. In this Habash was a
precursor for Khomeini.

The PFLP divided into several groups, its main
offshoot being the Popular Democratic Front for
the Liberation of Palestine (PDFLP) led by Nayef
Hawatmeh, who had worked against Habash while
he had been in a Syrian prison. Hawatmeh, a
Jordanian Bedouin Christian, also had an extreme
left revolutionary ideology, though he shared with
Habash nothing more than a hatred of the 'Conservative' Gulf states – Saudi Arabia, Jordan,
Kuwait and the various emirates. In this he too was
foreshadowing Khomeinism.

In 1968 a large new Syrian organization, called
the Vanguards of the Popular Liberation War, was
formed out of existing smaller groups. It soon
became the second biggest after Fatah; its military
arm was named Sa'iqa (Thunderbolt). Its declared
aim was a Palestinian state but this was to be
essentially part of a united Arab world under Syrian
leadership. Not to be outdone, Syria's Iraqi opponents formed the Arab Liberation Front (ALF),
which insisted that no state of Palestine should be
brought into existence because it would constitute
yet another division within the Arab world.

These major groups and many minor groups all paid lip service to the idea of martyrdom; in fact, some small groups included the word martyr in their titles. But neither the leadership nor their members proposed to become martyrs by suicide, as the Iranian and Lebanese Shi'a Muslims later did. Martyrdom by suicide was an alien concept to Sunnis and to the relatively small number of Christians in the terrorist organizations. Not infrequently a hijacker who had seized an aircraft *threatened* to blow himself up along with his hostages but such threats were never fulfilled.

In several instances terrorists on a raid into Israel to attack a kibbutz, hotel or school were killed in exchanges of fire with Israeli troops but the attackers were not members of suicide squads. Raiders from across the border could easily have driven a truck-bomb against an Israeli target – but this did not happen.

In their attacks on Israelis and on Westerners generally the PLO terrorists, from whatever group, knew that they ran the risk of being killed or wounded in a shoot-out with police or soldiers but they believed that the odds were heavily in favour of their being captured alive. Statistics support such a belief. Apart from this, Israel had no death penalty and there was always the possibility of release in a prisoner exchange. Not until 1985 did Sunni Muslims emulate Shi'a Muslims in attacks in which they had virtually no hope of surviving.

Habash was always closer to Shi'a Muslim thinking about the total nature of hostility towards the stated enemy than Arafat and other PLO leaders. I saw this sweeping aggression in 1972 when I told Habash that he could expect no international sympathy for his cause when his followers attacked innocent women and children and others who were in no way enemies of his. 'There is no such thing as an innocent person,' he said sharply. 'If you're alive you are involved.' He replied in this way to several journalists who brought up the notion of 'innocent people.' It always seemed strange to me that a Christian could hold such a view.

Habash had a similar conversation with the Italian journalist Oriana Fallaci in 1970 after Habash told her that he proposed to attack Israeli civilian aircraft. Miss Fallaci pointed out that the planes carried citizens of neutral countries who should not be considered as enemies.

Habash said:

The non-Israeli passengers are on their way to Israel. Since we have no control over the land, which is ours, it is right that whoever goes to Israel should ask our permission . . . We want a war just like the one in Vietnam . . . not just in Palestine but throughout the world . . . Our struggle has barely begun, the worst is yet to come. And it is right for Europe and America to be warned that there will be no peace . . .

The strategy and tactics which Habash outlined to Ms Fallaci were straight from Mao but his language was that of Islamic holy war – despite his Christian background.

Arafat's close friend and PFLP spokesman,

Gassan Kanafani, often brushed aside 'innocence' as an irrelevance and an illusion. A poet and a novelist, Kanafani told me in his office in Beirut, 'For as long as you are breathing you are in constant danger of ceasing to breathe. Innocence cannot protect anybody.' I was on my way to his office one day in the spring of 1972 when I heard that he had been killed by a bomb which blew up his car when he started the engine. A rival faction had murdered him. They also killed his 15-year-old niece in the blast; she was surely innocent.

After 1979 Arafat's thinking was influenced by Ayatollah Khomeini. The PLO leader was one of the first foreigners to go to Teheran following the overthrow of the Shah and the installation of Khomeini as the supreme imam of Iran. Much in Khomeini's company, he was impressed by his preaching of holy war and by the methods by which he proposed to wage that war. 'Martyrdom' was a fundamental part of it and Arafat realized that Khomeini was not merely indulging in rhetoric. 'Martyrs will conquer the world because the Satanic world [the West] has no way of countering it just as it cannot stop jihad,' Khomeini told Arafat, who later passed on this assertion to many of his associates.

However deeply Arafat was impressed by Khomeini, another terrorist leader, Sabri al-Banna – code-named Abu Nidal – had adopted holy war on the Shi'a Muslim model long before Khomeini returned to Iran from exile. This implacable advocate of 'revolutionary violence' – French journalist

Jean-Pierre Langellier calls him 'the symbol of blood and terror' – comes from a rich Jaffa Palestinian family. His father had several wives and one of them, a Syrian from Turkey, was Abu Nidal's mother. After 1948 Abu Nidal went to live in Saudi Arabia and was a youthful militant in an anti-monarchy movement. Arrested and expelled from Saudi Arabia, he began his 'real career' in Iraq where he formed a group operating under the name 'Black June' which broke with the PLO in 1972. From that time until 1980 he owed complete allegiance to Iraq and he primarily attacked Syrian and Jordanian interests. For instance, he planted bombs in the Semiramis and Intercontinental hotels in Amman and Damascus and the Syrian embassies in Italy and Pakistan.

In 1981 he broke with Iraq and opened an office in Syria; then he mended his relations with Iraq and for some time worked for both the opposing governments at the same time. He now called his group Fatah Revolutionary Command (no connection with Arafat's Fatah). He was expelled from Iraq in 1983 because President Saddam Hussein had evidence that Syria proposed to use Abu Nidal to murder him.

Fatah Revolutionary Command, under this name or others, has committed a long list of criminal attacks and has 'claimed' most of them. Most of Abu Nidal's victims are Arabs. One of the first was Yossef el Sibaah, editor-in-chief of *Al Ahram* and friend of President Sadat. He then killed Jordanian and Kuwaiti diplomats, representatives of other hated governments and Palestinian officials accused of 'treachery.' A prominent victim of this category was the moderate PLO leader Issam Sartawi, who had openly talked with leading men in Israeli's extreme left.

During 1985 Abu Nidal said that his organization had sentenced to death 'all those who have sought negotiations with the Zionist foe – with King Hussein heading the list – and executed dozens of persons.' The attacks against synagogues in Vienna in August 1981 and Rome in October 1982, the attempted murder of the Israeli ambassador in London in May 1982 and the August 1982 Rue de Rosiers (Paris) killings are among the crimes committed by Abu Nidal.

Interpol considers it easy to identify attacks by the Abu Nidal group. The savagery of the operations, the use of Soviet-made grenades and a favourite weapon – the Polish-made WZ-63 machine-pistol – are all hallmarks of the group. In any case, the group always uses the same form of language when claiming responsibility for its acts.

Abu Nidal claims that his organization is 'very strict, very severe and highly revolutionary.' At the same time he speaks of 'the inspiration of holy war.' However, Jean-Pierre Langellier, who has made a special study of Abu Nidal, says, 'Once stripped of its pseudo-Marxist verbiage, Abu Nidal's ideology can be reduced to a few phrases: 'Destroy the Zionist entity' (he never uses the word Israel), 'a people's war against Arab reactionaries'. He wants to wipe out everybody, Palestinians or other Arabs,

who want to negotiate with the enemy. As for Abu
Nidal's nationalism it is rather questionable. The
terrorist has never come out in favour of an independent Palestinian state. On the contrary, early
in 1985 he used to say, 'From every point of view
Palestine belongs to Syria. Like Lebanon it will be
part and parcel of it.'

Abu Nidal has also announced that he has a score
to settle with the Gulf emirates for having 'over-
looked' him when distributing financial assistance
to various Palestinian fronts.

Abu Nidal had always had Gaddafi's support,
along with other radical Palestinian groups, but
after Abu Nidal's final split in 1983 with the PLO
generally and Arafat's Fatah in particular he sought
Gaddafi's patronage. In September 1985 Abu Nidal
had discussions in Tripoli with Abdul Jalloud,
Gaddafi's deputy, and then with Gaddafi himself.
The result was that Gaddafi 'bought' Abu Nidal's
organization as a going concern for an annual
subsidy of $12 million. Gaddafi, whose own
Libyans are not martyr material, made it clear that
he expected Abu Nidal's men to be genuine holy
war warriors in the Shi'a Muslim mould and Abu
Nidal agreed.

When Abu Nidal and Gaddafi began to co-
operate on the extension of terrorism in Europe
they decided to use the emotional and religious
power of holy war in training the men who would
make the attacks. This was a logical step because
Western security against possible targets had
become more thorough, extensive and sophisti-

cated. There was no longer the high degree of
probability that the members of a hit squad would
survive. With this realization came the Nidal-
Gaddafi decision to induce Sunni Muslims to
accept martyrdom – when 'natural' Shi'a martyrs
were not available or were not willing to die in a
Nidal-Gaddafi attack.

The terrorists who took part in the massacres at
Rome and Vienna airports on 27 December 1985
had accepted martyrdom in the cause of holy war.
While they selected for attack the check-in desks
of the Israeli airline El Al, the killers knew that
people of other nationalities would be among the
passengers. Similarly, the El Al desks were close
to those of other airlines. The indiscriminate firing
of automatic rifles and throwing of grenades was a
hallmark of modern holy war. All the possible
victims are declared in advance to be 'enemies'.

The same outlook was evident when an Abu
Nidal group hijacked an Egyptian airliner to Malta
in November 1985. The day on which the aircraft
was seized was the Prophet Muhammad's traditional birthday; the hijack was therefore an act of
holy war – a 'present' for the Prophet. When
Egyptian commandos stormed the plane the terrorists threw grenades among the passengers, yet
again a declaration, in effect, that all were considered holy war enemies.

Arafat was well aware of the growing appeal of
holy war in the ranks of the PLO. Ever since the
organization's ejection from Lebanon, after it had
lost its war against Israel, the members had been

frustrated. All the Arab states among which its members were dispersed kept them unarmed and isolated while Palestinian communities in Lebanon were attacked by Lebanese Shi'a and Druse fighters. In one massacre perpetrated by Shi'as and Druse at Shatila and Sabra, Lebanon, in 1985 at least 1,500 Palestinians died. In camps in several Arab countries PLO men talked of holy war retaliation.

In mid-January 1986 Arafat perhaps unexpectedly found himself discussing holy war when he paid a visit to Riyadh to discuss finance for the PLO. Saudi Arabia is by far the PLO's most important benefactor, paying $20 million annually to keep the organization going. Arafat needed more money than ever because his groups were much dispersed. While his political headquarters remained in Tunis he had important military and administrative bases in Iraq, North Yemen and Jordan.

Despite much criticism of Arafat's leadership by many Arab leaders – the Syrians were trying to assassinate him in favour of the leader of the pro-Syrian faction of Fatah – Arafat found favour in Saudi Arabia. He was received by King Fahd and his brother Prince Salman, an honour which indicated the royal family's continued backing for his leadership. However, Arafat was told, Saudi Arabia expected him to make the PLO 'more Islamic.' Prince Salman conceded that he had shown a greater sense of Islamic responsibility in advocating holy war during his speech in Sudan but practice had to follow precept.

Some Arab observers felt that the Saudi leaders were playing with fire in pushing the PLO into a more militantly Islamic posture. Saudi Arabia itself was already under serious threat from holy war being preached and fought against them by Iran. However, the Saudis believe that as the PLO is impotent without their money its leaders might as well back Saudi Arabia in any holy war confrontation against the Syrians, Iranians and Saudi's own large Shi'a minority.

CHAPTER SIXTEEN
Searching for a defence

A radical Shi'a terrorist leader of Hezbollah living in Baalbek received a packet in the post one morning in October 1985. It had been posted in Beirut the day before and as it had none of the signs of a parcel bomb he opened it without fear. Out dropped a set of genitals – penis, testicles and scrotum. An accompanying note in Arabic briefly told the horrified recipient that the human parts had belonged to a relative of his but that he would not be needing them any more. In fact, after the victim had been castrated he had been shot in the head.

The Hezbollah official had been sent a gruesome message by the Russian KGB and it meant 'Do not kidnap and kill our people.' In September 1985 Hezbollah had kidnapped four Soviet diplomats in Beirut and held them hostage with the demand that Moscow put pressure on the Syrian government to stop shelling Muslim militia positions in the northern Lebanese city of Tripoli. The Syrians did not at once cease their attacks and the body of one of the kidnapped Russian diplomats, Arkady Katkov, was found a few days later. He had been shot in the head.

Following receipt of the genitals the Hezbollah kidnappers immediately released the three other

Russian hostages. A Lebanese journalist in Beirut told me, 'This is the way the Russians operate. They don't talk – they act. Hezbollah understands this language. Their terrorists do dreadful things to their captives but the Russian action against one of their own men shocked them.'

Islamic Jihad had always known that angering the Russians could be dangerous. In 1979, in Teheran, it seemed likely for at least a week that the mobs would storm the Soviet Embassy as they had the American Embassy. The Russians relayed a message direct to Ayatollah Khomeini that if the Soviet Embassy were to be violated 'ten ayatollahs would die suddenly.' Within hours a strong force of Revolutionary Guards was posted around the Soviet Embassy to protect it.

While the Soviet Union might have found a satisfactory response to certain aspects of the menace of holy war it eludes the rest of the world. Those Arab and other Islamic rulers and states which have been declared enemies and targets of holy war have no solution. President Sadat, commanding the most powerful army in the Arab world, could not protect himself when his attackers were members of that army. King Hussein, with probably the most loyal bodyguard of all Arab rulers, has nevertheless been the subject of numerous assassination attempts. The Saudi royal family was forced to hire élite Pakistani soldiers as bodyguards because their own Saudi soldiers were considered untrustworthy for such responsible duties.

There appears to be nothing the West can do to help Arab states and the Islamic world generally against the several different campaigns of holy war which engulf it. Nor would foreign attempts at peace-making be appreciated; they would be seen as intervention in the private affairs of Islam.

An interesting example of the way Islamic countries close ranks against what they call 'imperialist interference' or 'colonialist aggression' occurred in December 1985. Holy war terrorists had carried out at Rome and Vienna airports the massacres planned by Colonel Gaddafi in collusion with Abu Nidal. Among the victims were Americans and President Reagan assembled the US Sixth Fleet off the coast of Libya to indicate American anger. Gaddafi had only one friend among Arab rulers – President Assad of Syria – and few among the other score of Islamic leaders. Many Arabs and others would like to see him dead. Yet, at an Islamic summit conference coincidentally being held at that time, all 44 Islamic nations declared unanimously that they supported Libya and would come to its aid if the Americans attacked. Most would not have done so but the mere declaration of Islamic unity indicates the unanimity of purpose when confronting the Christian West.

Israel has tried several methods of protecting its citizens against the phenomenon of Shi'a Muslim suicide attack, a phenomenon which emerged in 1984. One tactic was to co-operate with the local Lebanese troops of the South Lebanese Army. Another was to erect sophisticated and expensive electronic and other defences along its border with Lebanon. Professor Etan Kohlberg, of the Hebrew University of Jerusalem and one of Israel's leading authorities on Shi'a Islam, declared that the only effective way for Israel to defend itself against the Iranian-inspired Shi'as was to 'disengage'; that is, for Israel to break completely from Lebanon.

He made this suggestion in March 1985 when the Israeli forces were already in the process of leaving Lebanon.

Kohlberg also had a novel suggestion. 'One could challenge the distorted religious concepts behind the present notion of suicide by having recourse to the Shi'as' own sacred texts. It would, in fact, be very easy to show that what they are doing is not gaining access to Paradise but engaging in a terrible sin. One would only have to cite the position of those of their own *ulema* (religious leaders) who are opposed, on strong religious grounds, to what is taking place.'

Kohlberg's idea would be worth trying but it is difficult to see how he or anybody else could reach the holy war leadership and induce them to listen to intellectual religious arguments against suicide attacks. While some members of the *ulema* oppose suicide among Muslims, for whatever reason, their voices are lost amid the rhetoric from the more charismatic and political-minded priests.

Another Israeli, Brigadier-General Gideon Mahanaimi, an expert on anti-terrorism, believes that holy war must not be fought only by military retaliation but by a comprehensive strategy including clandestine warfare, military action and diplomatic measures, In January 1986 he said, 'When we were able to kill one of the terrorist leaders there was a period of peace, but such killings are difficult to carry out. It takes time and requires co-operation with other countries. Israel has good co-operation with western intelligence services but there is room for improvement.'

Mahanaimi and other practical experts in the field suggest that closing of PLO offices, denying terrorists access to diplomatic pouches and boycotting countries that plan holy war operations and shelter terrorists could be effective. The same people admit that it is difficult to persuade countries to take these measures because of their own economic interests in the Islamic world. Islam is at the mercy of its own institutionalized violence and it faces other dangers, one of which was discerned by the great Orientalist Alfred Guillaume in a 1954 book on Islam. 'The old forces of reaction may be too strong for the new spirit of liberalism, armed as they are with shibboleths and anathemas which can arouse ignorant masses and terrorize men of vision. Only time can show which party will gain the upper hand.'

In the 1980s time has shown that the spirit of liberalism was dead. It has been strangled by the fundamentalists hell-bent on holy war.

European and American leaders dealing with holy war directed against their countries continually experience the frustration of not knowing with whom to negotiate in order to reach a peaceful relationship, to secure the release of hostages and to discuss disputes. The position of any Muslim who has offered himself as a mediator has always been ambiguous. For instance, during the attempts to arrange the release of the 40 American hostages held in Beirut after the hijacking of TWA flight 847 in June 1985, Nabih Berri put himself forward as a mediator. But as leader of the Shi'a Amal movement in Lebanon Berri supported the hijackers' demands and even added a condition of his own – that the American fleet should move away from the Lebanese coast.

Under first President Carter and then President Reagan the United States had been unable to mount an effective counter-offensive against holy war. The military operation to free the hostages in Teheran went wildly wrong; firing one-ton naval shells at vague targets in the Lebanese mountains achieved nothing; retribution and rescue operations were aborted or failed; protection of American installations abroad has been largely ineffective. The much-vaunted Delta Force, created and trained to deal with crises world-wide, could not respond to one hijack crisis because no aircraft were available to get the men to the spot.

Economic sanctions apparently achieve little. President Carter began to cut American links with Libya as early as 1978, when supplies of American military aircraft ended. In 1979 Libya was designated a country which had 'repeatedly supported international terrorism'; in 1980 the American embassy in Tripoli was closed; in 1982 the import of Libyan crude oil was stopped and in 1985 the purchase of refined oil products ceased as well. In 1986 President Reagan ended completely his country's links with Libya and announced punishments for Americans who arranged business deals with Libya in the future.

During 1985 the US National Security Council several times debated the almost desperate 'solution' of abducting terrorists who harm American citizens and taking them back to the United States to stand trial.

The turning point in the US attitude to anti-terrorist warfare came in October 1985 when the Americans 'bent' international law by seizing the PLO pirates who had taken over the Italian cruise liner *Achille Lauro*. When the ship put into Port Said the pirates gave themselves up to the Egyptian authorities but by then they had killed an American hostage. The Egyptians provided the PLO pirates, who included Abu Abbas, the leader of the Palestine Liberation Front, with a getaway plane. Over the Mediterranean this plane was intercepted by American fighter aircraft and forced to land in Sicily, where the pirates were arrested. The Italians permitted Abu Abbas to move on to Yugoslavia but his gang was imprisoned.

In January 1986 the US State Department's chief legal adviser, Abraham Sofaer (in an interview in the *New York Times*) said that the department was prepared to support the 'seizure' of fugitives in other countries if the chances of success were reasonable. The Justice Department had already issued arrest warrants for the hijackers of the TWA airliner.

Arguments against American efforts to seize terrorists are strong. For instance, dangerous legal precedents could be set and there could be problems with European allies. There are fears also that abduction efforts could go wrong, leading perhaps to unnecessary loss of life.

The Times (9.1.1986) advised those who might want to take forceful action against Libya following the Rome and Vienna massacres that 'If military action is appropriate it should be surgical and swift – and carried out against the Abu Nidal bases deep in Libya.' The principle of being surgical and swift should apply to all bases from which holy war is launched.

The Economist (11.1.1986) saw no moral objection to meeting force with force. 'The Americans should not rule out the possibility of military action when Libyans are once again caught somewhere with a smoking gun and those of America's allies that have the right sort of military power – notably Britain, France and West Germany – should be ready to help. The trouble with the military option is that it is difficult to put into practice with the necessary precision.'

The Economist believed that the United States was right to try to persuade Europe to impose wider diplomatic sanctions. 'European governments, at first, will not listen to America. But public opinion in Europe is more friendly – and more down to earth. Sooner rather than later

Libyan fingerprints will be found on another batch of corpses. Then sanctions might begin to make more obvious sense.'

After Britain imposed tight restrictions on visas for Libyans in 1984 and monitored more closely the movements of those who filtered through the net the activities of Gaddafi's hit squads were contained.

The best argument for the increased use of anti-terrorist force is its deterrent effect. US Secretary of State George Schultz outlined the rationale most bluntly in October 1984 when he said, 'We cannot allow ourselves to become the Hamlet of nations, worrying endlessly over whether and how to respond.'

Apart from Delta Force the US has trained a variety of military units in tactics against holy war attackers. They include the Army's helicopter unit Task Force 168, the Navy's SEALS (for Sea; Air and Land forces) and the Air Force's First Special Operations Wing. West Germany has its GSG 9 group. All are based on the techniques and tactics of Britain's SAS.

Robert Kupperman, a senior adviser at George-town's Center for Strategic and International Studies, is an advocate of pre-emptive covert war against holy war. This would include air strikes against Islamic Jihad, Shi'a Amal, Libyan, PLO and other bases, and selective assassination. These methods have their problems. *The Washington Post* revealed that in 1984 President Reagan approved a covert CIA operation to train and

support counter holy war groups in the Middle
East. About four months later, according to the
Post, members of a Lebanese counter-offensive
unit, acting without CIA authorization, hired
another band of Lebanese gunmen to detonate a
car bomb outside the Beirut residence of Sheikh
Muhammad Fadlallah, one of the key planners
behind the suicide bombings of the US Marine
headquarters and the US embassy annex in Beirut.
In this unapproved car bombing 80 people were
killed – but Fadlallah was unharmed.

The French had understood the problem of
precise military action for some years. With four
hostages – two diplomats and two journalists – in
Iran they had studied scores of military possibilities
for rescuing them and abandoned all of them.
Finally, President Mitterand and his government
were reduced to serious consideration of paying
the one billion dollar ransom demanded by Iran for
the four hostages.

The Archbishop of Canterbury's foreign affairs
adviser, Mr Terry Waite, has shown that it is
possible, under certain exceptional circumstances,
to negotiate with Islamic holy war leaders. He
secured the freedom of missionaries detained in
Iran and other hostages held in Libya and Lebanon, after months of patient and persistent dealing.
Then he himself became a hostage in January 1987.
Mr Waite showed great personal courage but his
successes were not the result of his persuasive
eloquence; they came about because Ayatollah

Khomeini and Colonel Gaddafi saw a political
advantage in handing over their hostages. Modern
teaching of holy war in Islam insists that at all times
the advantage must lie with Islam. 'He who deals
with the West,' Ayatollah Khomeini announced in
1984, 'must be able to prove that he does so for the
benefit of Islam.' This statement is likely to become
one of the principal holy war axioms.

Much-publicized attacks on Israeli targets might
well give the impression that Israel is the major
target for holy war but it ranks fairly low in Islamic
Jihad's order of priority. Israel's geographical close-
ness to Middle Eastern Islam is another factor in
producing the erroneous notion that it is the principal holy war enemy. Certain Arabs as well as
Western Christians precede Jews in the thinking of
jihad's planners. Some of them link Christians and
Jews as indivisible.

According to a hitherto secret report, apparently
drawn up in part by Ayatollah Fazollah Mahalati, a
senior official of the holy war command in Teheran,
jihad's priorities in 1986 ran in this order:

1 Iraq
2 The Arab monarchies
3 Egypt
4 The United States
5 Western Europe, particularly France and
    Britain
6 Israel
7 The black African states. Some, such as Zaire,
    are 'enemies'; others, such as Rwanda,

southern Sudan and Central African Republic are priorities for conversion to Islam.
8 Turkey
9 Spain
10 The Muslim states of the Soviet Union.

Even for the Lebanese Shi'a members of Hezbollah Israel is only third in line after the United
States and France. Gaddafi's list of priorities might
be rather different but the United States, Egypt,
black Africa and his own 'traitors' would precede
Israel. Yasser Arafat's part of the PLO would
probably place Israel at the top of its list but the
Syrian-controlled PLO would give this position to
Arafat himself. Abu Nidal's priorities are similar to
those of Gaddafi with the exception of King Hussein of Jordan, who heads the Nidal list. Also, black
Africa is low on the Abu Nidal list.

For Pakistan, the intellectual-academic centre
for holy war, a list of priorities would make little
sense. There is simply *Dar al-Harb*, the region of
war or non-Islamic world, which must gradually be
brought into *Dar al-Islam*. The over-riding concern
of Pakistan's religious leaders is the world-wide
presentation of Islam through information and
propaganda.

'Experts' on holy war readily pronounce on the
seriousness of the situation but nobody has effective counter-measures. At the end of 1985 Professor Paul Wilkinson of the University of Aberdeen
said, 'We may be entering an entirely new phase
in which fanatics will stop at nothing, killing for the

pure joy of blowing themselves up along with innocent passengers.' The 'pure joy' can be conceded; Hussein Mussawi told me about that. Equally, the 'innocent passengers' *cannot* be conceded; a score of holy war publicists have told me that 'innocence' is non-existent when applied to non-Islamic people.

After a lengthy seminar in Washington on ways to respond to the dangers of holy war, Admiral James Watkins of the US Joint Chiefs-of-Staff expressed the difficulty in a more succinct and realistic way than most. 'We don't know how to deal with it because they win if they live and they win if they die.'

The zealots of Islam believe that Christianity is in its failing phase. An Egyptian scholar who is also a traditionalist revolutionary told me, 'This is the period of post-Christianity, and Judaism is no obstacle, except in the temporary stumbling-block of Israel. During the next twenty years we can make Islam supreme over the West.' He was speaking in 1970.

The Muslim writer Muhammad al-Mutti Bakhit wrote in 1926, 'The Islamic religion is based on the pursuit of domination and power and strength and might.' The men of Islamic Jihad and its associated common-interest groups from many parts of the Muslim world are demonstrating their acceptance of this viewpoint as they press on with their holy war.

In December 1984 the Speaker of the Iranian parliament, Ayatollah Hashemi-Rafsanjani, made a statement which, in condensed form, expressed the views of the academics, such as Bakhit and A'bul Maududi, and the military teachings of Brigadier Malik. In his textbook on the *Koranic* concept of war Malik had written, 'Terror is . . . not only the means but the end in itself.' Rafsanjani's statement was just as direct. 'If our wishes are not granted we shall drag you into a sea of fire and blood. We shall be at war with you, hitting you everywhere.'

One of the methods by which the Iranians and their holy war allies intend to hit their 'satanic' enemies did not become clear until early 1986 when it was learned that Iranian pilots had been trained to fly light planes loaded with explosives on suicide missions. Their targets were US warships in the Mediterranean and land facilities throughout the Middle East.[1]

The Shi'a kamikaze force is potentially far more dangerous than the hijackers and suicide car bombers. Only the continuation of Iran's war with Iraq had kept the Khomeini regime, up till 1987, from sending suicide pilots against American targets. These fliers, mostly volunteers, were first trained on powered gliders in the Syrian-controlled Bekaa Valley of eastern Lebanon. The Syrians bought these gliders from West German firms in 1981–82, intending to lend them to Palestinian guerrillas. However the 1982 split between the Syrians and

[1] During World War II Japanese suicide or kamikaze pilots destroyed 36 American warships and damaged 368 in just one battle in the Pacific – that of Okinawa – in 1945.

the Palestine Liberation Organization ended that scheme.

The Syrians then offered the gliders to the Iranian Revolutionary Guards who were eager to form a kamikaze force but they were not satisfied with the performance of the German gliders, which they thought were too slow and too vulnerable to deflection by wind. After a study by Iranian and Syrian experts, the Iranian government bought 80 Swiss Pilatus PC7 aircraft in 1984. These aircraft are generally used for crop dusting and the Iranians assured the Swiss that they would indeed be used in agriculture and for rescue missions and pilot training.

The Swiss became alarmed when they discovered that the technical documents sent to Iran with the PC7s included instructions on how to convert them into warplanes. But by now the kamikaze pilots had begun training at Bushire, the main Iranian fighter-bomber airbase on the Persian Gulf. Later some were sent to Won San, North Korea, for further training. Several volunteers were killed in accidents during low-level flight exercises. One of the survivors was Hushang Mortezai, who defected and fled to London where he went into hiding.

Mortezai told Western intelligence officers who debriefed him that he knew of no other defectors among the kamikaze fliers. 'My comrades are wholly fanatical,' he said. 'They are preparing to make their strikes and nothing will stop them. It is just a matter of when the time is considered right.'

The German gliders, whose use has not been abandoned, and the PC7s may be able to evade the US warships' radar protection. On land it would be virtually impossible to protect American embassies and other possible targets against airborne suicide attack. Islamic Jihad has shown that it has the ability, the means and above all the will to sustain holy war for a long time.

Spelling and Glossary

For the sake of simplicity I spell Arabic words and
names as they are commonly used in leading
English-language newspapers and journals. Hence,
I use Koran rather than Qur'an and President
Nasser (Nasir). I prefer Muslim to the equally used
Moslem and Muhammad to Mohammad mainly
because there is no letter 'o' in the Arabic alphabet.
I have omitted most of the many dascritical marks
such as accents and apostrophes which appear in
transliterated Arabic.

'Abd (slave)   Common in names – Abdullah.
Allah   The Arabic word for God, used by Christian
   Arabs as well as Muslims.
Amal (hope)   One of the Lebanese Shi'a extremist
   groups.
Ashure   The tenth day of the month of Muharram
   in the Islamic calendar. It is a day of mourning,
   especially among Shi'a Muslims, commemorat-
   ing the death of the Prophet's grandson, the
   Imam Hussein.
assassin   Historically, the name of an extremist
   Muslim sect, a branch of the Ismailis; in their
   time the Assassins were a dangerous threat to all
   established order – religious, political and social.
ayatollah   A high-ranking Muslim cleric – though

strictly speaking Islam does not have a hierarchy of clergy.

Caliph (successor)   The representative of God on earth and therefore the successor of the Prophet Muhammad. The title was first held by Arab and then by Ottoman rulers until the final overthrow of the Ottoman Caliphate after World War 1.

Dar al-Harb   The areas of mankind still unsubdued to Islam; 'the house of war.'

Dar al-Islam   The 'house of Islam,' the actual realm of the Muslim faith in which Islam is in full political and religious control.

dhimmi   A non-Muslim living under a 'covenant' (dhimma) with special obligations to a Muslim government. A dhimmi is a second-class citizen who buys protection by paying a special tax.

fard ala'l-kifaya   A duty imposed on men to assemble for holy war.

hadith (communication or narrative)   The body of verbal or written traditions concerning the words and deeds of the Prophet Muhammad and his companions. Also, a single one of these traditions.

Hajj or Hadjdj   The pilgrimage to Mecca in the sacred month.

hegira or hidjra (breaking of relations or emigration)   The Prophet Muhammad's flight from Mecca to Medina in A.D. 622 is the date from which the Muslim era is counted.

imam   The temporal and spiritual ruler of Islam; a title of the Caliph. Also, a leader in prayer at mosques.

Islam The act of surrendering oneself to Allah;
literally the verb form of islam means to deliver
over in sound condition. The common definition
of islam is submission.

jihad or djihad Muslim holy war against unbelievers whether pagan, Christian or Jew. Holy war
is a duty of Muslims in general.

Kaba (cube) The most important place of worship
in Mecca.

Koran (reading or recitation) The holy book of
Islam, revealed by the angel Gabriel to
Muhammad.

mahdi (guided one) Name taken by various
Islamic leaders who claimed divine
enlightenment.

Mecca Muhammad's birthplace in Saudi Arabia,
the site of the Kaba and the holy mosque.

Medina The city to which Muhammad and his
followers migrated in A.D. 622. Muhammad died
and was buried at Medina.

mudjahidun or mujahideen (sing. mudjahid; fighters for the faith) Originally, the fighters in holy
wars, in contemporary Middle East Islam
especially Iran, nationalist guerrillas.

mufti A qualified 'lawyer' able to give a legal
opinion on the Shari'a; a person of considerable
rank.

mullah A prayer leader, generally lower in status
than an ayatollah or hojetelislam.

Muslim Legalistically a Muslim, a follower of
Islam, is one who says, 'I witness that there is no

Allah but Allah, and Muhammad is the messenger of Allah.'

Pasdaran   The Revolutionary Guards of Iran.

Ramadan   The ninth month of the Muslim lunar calendar in which the Koran was first revealed to Muhammad; observed by fasting and abstinence during daylight hours.

rukn   A fundamental duty of Muslims.

shahada   The profession of faith, a statement of the fundamental belief in Islam: 'There is no god but God and Muhammad is His Messenger.'

shaheed   The Muslim word for a man who has died as a martyr.

Shari'a (clear path)   The law of Islam.

Shi'a or Shi'ite (partisan)   A follower of the Muslim sect which rejects the first three Caliphs and the authority of the sunna. Shi'as say that Ali should have become caliph on Muhammad's death.

Sufi   A follower of a system of Islamic contemplative life.

sunna or sunnah (custom, usage or statute)   The orthodox code of Islamic practice transmitted through Muhammad's immediate successors.

sura   One of the 114 chapters of the Koran.

ulama or ulema (pl. of alim)   Theologians who rule on important religious and political matters.

umma   The Islamic community of believers.

zakat   Originally not so much a tax as an alms-giving. By giving alms a Muslim is purified.

Index